LEARNING
TO
SURVIVE

LEARNING TO SURVIVE

Black Youth Look for Education and Hope

Atron A. Gentry
with Carolyn C. Peelle

Foreword by *Bill Cosby*

AUBURN HOUSE
Westport, Connecticut
London

Library of Congress Cataloging-in-Publication Data

Gentry, Atron.
  Learning to survive : Black youth look for education and hope /
Atron A. Gentry with Carolyn C. Peelle; foreword by William H. Cosby, Jr.
    p. cm.
  Includes bibliographical references and index.
  ISBN 0–86569–207–6 (alk. paper)—ISBN 0–86569–261–0 (pbk. : alk. paper)
    1. Afro-American youth—Education.   2. Socially handicapped youth—
Education—United States.   3. Gangs—United States.   4. Education,
Urban—United States.   I. Peelle, Carolyn C.   II. Title.
LC2717.G45   1994
370'.8996073—dc20   93–49637

British Library Cataloguing in Publication Data is available.

Library of Congress Catalog Card Number: 93–49637
ISBN: 0–86569–207–6
     0–86569–261–0 (pbk.)

First published in 1994

Auburn House, 88 Post Road West, Westport, CT 06881
An imprint of Greenwood Publishing Group, Inc.

Printed in the United States of America

∞™

The paper used in this book complies with the
Permanent Paper Standard issued by the National
Information Standards Organization (Z39.48–1984).

10 9 8 7 6 5 4 3 2 1

Copyright Acknowledgments

The authors and publisher gratefully acknowledge permission to reprint the following
copyrighted material:

Extracts from "Boston Secondary Schools Project: A Successful School-University
Collaboration," in *The Teacher Educator*, 27:2, Autumn 1991, pp. 9–19.

Extracts from "Urban School/University Collaboration: The Boston Secondary Schools
Project," in *American Secondary Education*, 20:4, 1992, pp. 24–29.

To my grandchildren, Yahn and Caylin

Contents

❏ ❏ ❏

Foreword

❑ ❑ ❑

Good. You're reading this book. *Learning to Survive* is important. If you walk down any Main Street, U.S.A., and ask the people you meet, "How important is education?" they will say—almost to a person—that it's the most important thing we do. Because we all care about our children.

I've worked with children in many settings, and the amazing thing about little kids is that they all start out smart and hopeful (and usually giggling). So, that's the *easy* part about educating our kids. They're ready. The *hard* part—for teachers, principals, school boards, professors, and politicians—is that, in the fall, with each new kindergarten class, you have to start the job of educating all over again.

We've had this cycle in education of continually pulling the plug: pouring resources into good programs, then cutting them for no good reason, and then saying, "Can anybody think of a good program?" We empty the water out of the bathtub and then try to figure out how to fill it up again. Sooner or later, the adults charged with the task grow tired and discouraged—because they have to keep filling up the tub.

But the kids don't know this. The five year old who shows up for school the first day—new sweater, shiny lunch box, big smile, and speaking in two languages—he doesn't know Mrs. Sweet is all tired out from refilling the bathtub thirty-seven times already.

Nevertheless, we have to remember we're the adults here. It's the same with older kids who join gangs. We adults have known for forty years what drives them out of schools, out of their homes, on to the streets and into gangs. I'm reminded of what Maxine Waters said about rap performers and their "shocking" language: Instead of kicking them out, "let us embrace them," and hold on to them no matter how hard they fight us. We are the adults, and we should be able to understand them, teach them, and help them see the future.

When I first met Atron Gentry at the University of Massachusetts in the early 1970s, he was talking about "The Hope Factor" and how even the hardest gang members wanted an education. Every time I've seen him since, I've asked, "Are you still talking about The Hope Factor?" And Atron says, "Oh, you remember??!!"

Hope is as natural as breathing. We use the word all the time—sometimes very casually, as in:

"I'll be back later."

"I hope so."

"Say, Man, I think we've run out of gas."

"I hope not."

Or, after you have forgiven your child for doing something incredible, then comes "The Hope Factor," and you say:

"I *hope* you won't do that again."

One day in 1946 I was down in the basement with my paternal grandfather, watching him fix the furnace, and he shared some basic life philosophy with me. He said, "Bill, you've got to remember the three H's in life: Hope, Help, and Hurt."

Hope—everybody needs it to survive. That's what keeps you going. That's what keeps people buying lottery tickets, too. You say, "The odds against winning are eight million to one." And they say, "I'll take two, please." In real life situations, the odds might be bad, but you'll never make it without hope.

Help—well that's what everybody needs at some point. When you run out of energy, time or resources, you need some *help*. And when people don't get help or see no help coming, they lose hope and feel angry or frustrated. They might even decide to disregard rules or laws.

Then, my grandfather explained, "Someone is going to get hurt."

Again, we have to remember we are the adults here. Sometimes fear or propaganda makes people blind to that. Atron wrote about seeing Los Angeles police stop, search, and rough up a ten-year-old boy who "was just a baby." When we look at each other through the eyes of fear, we forget who's the child and who's the adult. Yes, we do need to "take away the guns and give them books"—or computers, or violins, or tennis rackets, or telescopes. We do need to help our children.

Now, think about a pin-ball machine. The ball rolls at a certain speed. It bounces off lights and bumpers. The machine is tilted down toward the player. The ball reaches its maximum height and starts to fall. The player tries to beat gravity and time.

When you pull back the plunger, the first ball is released. The bumpers kick it up and down randomly. But still, there is a force beyond luck: you, the player. Just near the end, where the ball falls lowest, are the flippers—your most powerful weapon. The final score depends on your skill and how badly you want to keep the ball in play. If you haven't practiced or get bored or distracted, the ball will fall down the hole quicker. You still get a score, just by the luck of the bounces; but if you really care and know how to use the flippers, you can hit that 100,000 point bumper!

Now, Atron writes that most educational researchers don't want simple answers for complex problems. They would say: "Observe the ratio between the inclination of the pin-ball machine and the velocity of the metal ball, divided by the acceleration of the terminal flippers, all multiplied by the angle of incidence.... " But I just want to say: "It depends on how badly you want to keep the ball in play. And, are you going to be the player? Or the pin-ball?"

The research in this book addresses complex problems using the power of simplicity. Atron tells the stories of street gang members and simply says, "These are America's children. They want a chance like anyone else. We all need hope."

Atron writes as an education professor and as a black male raised up and schooled in America. *Learning to Survive* shows us school and street truths, from both the inside and the outside.

Ever since I met Atron, I have admired how he creates hope in his life and his work. He has always kept a shy distance, respecting my celebrity. I am very, very proud to contribute to this book and to be a part of "The Hope Factor."

William H. Cosby, Jr.
Ed.D.

Acknowledgments

❑ ❑ ❑

I would like to thank the gang members and former gang members in the Los Angeles and Oakland, California, areas who allowed me to interview them. At Pace School in Los Angeles, Director Sharon Roberts and teachers Cedric Anderson and Sandy Osborn invited me to observe the program and talk to students and staff. I thank them for that opportunity.

Several colleagues at the University of Massachusetts, Amherst, School of Education provided feedback for this undertaking; particularly Drs. Byrd Jones, Norma Jean Anderson and Richard Clark. Special thanks to those of our urban education graduates—still working in the trenches—who read and commented on final drafts: Dr. Roscoe Cook, Dr. William Dearman, Dr. Harold Hutchins, Dr. Charles Jenkins, Dr. Dale McCollum, and Dr. Jack Woodbury. My friend and colleague, Herbert Pierce, provided invaluable assistance with data, editing and reality checks.

A very special thanks to my coauthor, Dr. Carolyn Peelle. We first began working together in 1969 while founding the Center for Urban Education at the University of Massachusetts. In the ensuing twenty-five years, there have been few articles, doctoral dissertations or research reports that have escaped her pen.

Atron A. Gentry
Amherst, Massachusetts

LEARNING
TO
SURVIVE

chapter one

America's Children in Crisis

❏ ❏ ❏

CHILDREN ARE THE FUTURE

They are tomorrow's adults—the next generation who will go to work, raise families, buy houses, vote in elections, perhaps go off to war. Doesn't everyone believe that children are the future? Why, then, does it appear that no one cares about so many of America's children?

We begin our story about gangs, education and hope for urban youth with these alarming facts:

- Children constitute the largest group living in poverty in this country.

- Over half of all black children will live below the poverty line at some point during their childhood years.

- Today, a boy born in Bangladesh has a longer life expectancy than an African American boy born in the United States.

- Infant mortality rates in the United States have improved, but we still rank twentieth out of forty developed countries.

- A black baby is twice as likely as a white baby to die during its first year.

- Our childhood immunization rate ranks below that of many third world countries.

- In 1989, there were 2.2 million cases of reported child abuse, three times the number reported twenty years ago.

- Homicide is the leading cause of death among black youth.
- On a typical day, forty children are injured or killed by gunshot wounds.
- Between 1985 and 1990, juvenile homicide increased five times faster than adult homicide. In the past five years, arrests for homicides among juveniles have gone up almost 100 percent.
- Suicides for teens aged 15 to 19 years tripled between 1960 and 1988 from 3.6 to 11.3 per 100,000.[1]

Enough? There's more.

The backdrop for the plight of our nation's inner-city children is the overall deterioration of social well-being in this country during the past twenty years. Yes, things have gotten worse! The "U.S. Index of Social Health," published by Fordham University's Institute for Innovation in Social Policy, has fallen to its lowest point in thirty years. Measuring seventeen areas of social well-being—such as children in poverty, unemployment, homicides, high school dropouts or the gap between rich and poor—the index dropped from a high of 71.8 points in 1976, to less than 40 points throughout the 1980s, with a low of 32.9 in 1989 (reported in *The Daily Hampshire Gazette*, Northampton, Mass., January 9, 1992 p. 1). Three problems were reported to be at their worst level: child abuse, teen suicide and the chasm between rich and poor. Twelve of the seventeen measured categories have worsened in the past twenty years.

Another index, the well-being of children in America, reported a decline in six of the nine measures taken. In March 1992, the Annie E. Casey Foundation and the Center for the Study of Social Policy reported that American children grew poorer during the 1980s, were more likely to become criminals or crime victims and were less likely to live with two parents (reported in *The New York Times*, March 24, 1992 A22).

Nationwide, the number of children living in poverty increased by 22 percent, births to single teenagers rose 14 percent, children in single-parent families increased 13 percent, violent deaths of teenagers increased 11 percent, juvenile incarceration rose 10 percent and babies born with low birth weight rose 3 percent.

Although some indices improved, such as overall infant mortality, the median income of families with children fell by 5 percent.

Parents worked harder and earned less, while having less time to care for their children. Overall, from 1979 to 1990, the average income of families in the bottom fifth income bracket fell 12.6 percent, while the average income of families in the top fifth increased 9.2 percent.

That last set of figures tells the most important story. Because more black families' earnings are in the bottom fifth (37 percent versus only 14.2 percent of whites), and because fewer black families' earnings are in the top fifth (14.5 percent versus 32.5 percent for whites), those recent shifts in wealth have had a disproportionate negative impact on black children (Hacker 1992).

Since 1973, the median income of all young families with children plunged by one-third. The earnings of the heads of young, black families with children fell 71 percent—from $13,860 to $4,030 in 1990 dollars. The median income of young black families is now below the federal poverty line for a family of three (Edelman 1992). Even when black children live in a family whose income exceeds the poverty level, that family is more likely than a white family to consist of both parents working full-time.

Those figures tell about the plight of those who *have* jobs. The crisis of black children growing up in poverty has multiple causes, but none is more important than the high rates of unemployment and underemployment for black men. Since the 1950s, unemployment rates for black males have consistently been double those for whites. White Americans have been unable to imagine or grasp the implications of that economic disaster. They only need to ask their grandparents: In the Great Depression of the 1930s, unemployment in white America reached an all-time high of 24.9 percent. Families broke up, men committed suicide, mental health problems and alcoholism soared; the homeless were everywhere. Yet, as Michael E. Connor noted in his chapter in Gibbs' *Young, Black, and Male in America*, "Underemployment and unemployment among 'freed' black males in the United States have never been lower than 24.9 percent and white America continues to show little understanding, compassion, or concern for this issue" (Gibbs 1988, 193).

Increasingly, relative poverty and deterioration of other conditions have made a bad situation worse in many urban communities. Look at Los Angeles, California, the Mecca of economic dreams and new hope for many Americans and for thousands of foreign immigrants who moved there. My professional journey as an educator and a community organizer began in the Los Angeles area in the 1960s. There were many tough problems in unemployment, education, and racial tension that I and others addressed in our community work. Gangs were a strong lure for youth then as well as now. However, in the 1960s, many youth could graduate from gangs to adult work. There were more community programs and athletic opportunities. Schools could offer a ticket to the mainstream if you were persistent. Black people worked hard to survive, but most could survive.

Today, the poverty rate in parts of Los Angeles is higher than at the time of the Watts riots in 1965. The gang members I interviewed for this book in October 1991, shortly before the Los Angeles uprising the following spring, faced a more hopeless future and far more dangerous streets than the young men I worked with in 1965. Los Angeles at the time of this writing still languishes in a three-year recession. In poor black neighborhoods, unemployment is as high as 50 percent. In South Central Los Angeles, home to the original "Crips" and "Bloods" gangs, more than 70,000 jobs disappeared in the 1970s and 1980s. There are more than 100,000 estimated gang members in Los Angeles County, alone.

A year after the Los Angeles riots, Richard Lacayo wrote a portrait of the city's "Unhealed Wounds" for *Time Magazine*. Hopes for federal and state funds to help rebuild the neighborhoods had not been realized. The school system groaned under a $400 million debt. "Not since Chicago in the 1930s has a city been held hostage by such a large army of street gangs" (*Time Magazine*, April 19, 1993).

The young men who make up those gangs were children just yesterday. They were born to parents struggling to survive economically, often an overworked single parent—children who likely faced health problems and emerged from childhood onto dangerous streets without much refuge at home or school.

These are America's children. Their futures are not bright. Yet their futures are a part of all our futures. We seem to have forgotten, or never noticed, them. The journalist, Leon Bing, interviewed members of the Crips and Bloods in her book *Do or Die*. She was asked later how she could even report such violent, "monstrous acts." She answered:

It was a monstrous act. But these kids are not monsters. They are growing against all odds in poisonous soil. I cannot judge them. And I cannot fix it for them, this horrible world they live in. . . . These are American kids. Nobody cares about them. We are so obsessed with the rights of the unborn, but we don't care about these kids after they are born. They are not just social aberrations. They are children, and they are being ground into dust. (*Time Magazine*, March 16, 1992, 17)

For the children of South Central Los Angeles and other ghettos like it, "Childhood has become a dangerous condition," as Malcolm-Jamal Warner said in the PBS Special "Gangs: Dreams Under Fire" (PBS, Channel 57, September 15, 1993). One boy explained, "I was first shot at when I was 9 years old. It's . . . like surviving in a jungle." Said Warner, "A young person without hope is a dangerous thing."

On almost every well-being dimension, poor children are faring poorly, and none so poorly or at risk as young black males—actually described as "An Endangered Species" (Gibbs 1988). Homicide is the leading cause of death for young black males. Over 4,000 teenagers were killed in this country in 1993. The United States' homicide rate for young men is four to seventy-three times that of other developed nations: twenty-two deaths per 100,000 in males 15 to 24 years old. The rate for whites is thirteen per 100,000 and for blacks, an incredible eighty-five per 100,000! In *Deadly Consequences*, Dr. Deborah Prothrow-Stith describes this phenomenon as neither natural nor inevitable, but a public health problem to be approached like an epidemic (Prothrow-Stith 1991).

Young black men serving in the military commit murder at lower rates than whites in the military. By contrast, the setting for civilian epidemic killing is poverty, danger and overcrowding—and, the ready availability of guns. When whites are just as poor and overcrowded, they murder at the same high rate in this country. Most whites and others who greatly fear black street youth do not realize that, although black men do commit almost half of all murders recorded, in 94 percent of cases, both victim and assailant are black. Of the more than 25,000 homicides in 1990, 70 percent were blacks killed by other blacks. In at least half the homicides, the people know each other. These grim facts are just a part of the larger picture in a country where 115,107 people were murdered by guns in the past decade, 86,749 of them by handguns (Jon Katz, "The War at Home," in *Rolling Stone*, July 8, 1993).

These terrible statistics weigh us down with a kind of disbelief. We can only understand them by imagining a young man with a name and a face and a mother who mourns his death. Imagine how the residents of these inner-city war zones have become numb, even fatalistic. "What you and I read about in the headlines, hundreds of thousands of ordinary kids are living every day, often without the protection or guidance of any adult" (Prothrow-Stith 1991, 24). Some gang members I interviewed wore pre-paid cemetery plot tags around their necks. Some young gang members won't even duck down in a drive-by shooting. Another dimension of the relentless danger of the streets for young black men is the danger of police violence. Between 1976 and 1987, approximately 1,800 black persons and 3,000 whites were killed by law enforcement officers (Hacker 1992).

When presenting statistics about robbery, journalists and criminologists rarely note that the street crimes by poor people are much more likely to result in arrest (or death) than the more middle-class crimes such as shoplifting, embezzlement or fraud. Department stores report that their greatest losses are from employees' theft (Hacker 1992). The most sophisticated white-collar crimes, such as those in the savings and loan scandals, often go unpunished and pay very well.

Before shifting our focus from the dangers for black youth to society's punishments, we have to examine the role of guns—ever more powerful guns—in the epidemic of violence in inner cities and elsewhere. Young people of all races are committing more murders and other serious crimes than ever before, but the *number* of young people engaged in such crimes has not grown in the last ten or twenty years. (That number peaked in the early 1970s according to a report from *The New York Times*, September 13, 1992.) Studies show that 50 to 60 percent of all crime is being committed by 5 to 7 percent of young people from the ages of ten to twenty. The erupting violence of the 1980s coincides with the dramatic rise in the use of crack cocaine and with the dramatic increase in the availability of firearms. The F.B.I. found that the number of killings committed by youths with firearms in the 1980s rose 79 percent ("On Meaner Streets, the Violent Are More So," *The New York Times*,

September 13, 1992, 6). Arguments and disputes that used to be settled by fists or knives are now usually settled by hand guns.

Beyond the high risks of poverty, ill health, and danger on the streets for American black children is the very high risk of going to jail. Making a fair appraisal of black youth delinquency is not easy. Criminologist Richard Dembo (in Gibbs' *Young, Black and Male in America: An Endangered Species*) cautions that we need to compare delinquency rates of similar socioeconomic groups of youth and to look at incidence as well as prevalence. Further, we need to compare official police reports with self-reports of delinquent activity.

Taking all these factors into account, Dembo summarizes that the higher rates of assault, robbery and murder for black male youths almost even out when similar SES (socioeconomic status) groups are compared. However, there are some important differences. Prevalence, that is, total numbers of persons involved in delinquent behavior, appear very similar for black versus white low- and working-class SES youth. Incidence, that is, the number of illegal activities, appears greater among low-income black juveniles. One explanation is that the environmental setting in inner-city ghettos creates more common delinquency. Delinquent white youth in similar situations are more heavily into substance abuse and generally more alienated from mainstream society. "The white male youth who engaged in delinquent behavior in degree and type sufficient to bring them to the attention of juvenile justice agencies appear to have moved a greater psychological and ethical distance than the black youth, who, perhaps, come from environmental settings in which delinquency is more prevalent and, hence, regarded as less unacceptable by their peers" (Gibbs 1988, 159).

Finally, there is consistent evidence that black youth are proportionally overrepresented in the processing activities of various juvenile justice system agencies—from point of arrest through incarceration. The discrepancy persists when race and SES are considered together:

The issue of bias in the juvenile justice system, reflected in the disproportionate rates of arrest for black male youth, their placement in detention centers, and commitment to public juvenile correctional facilities, requires immediate action. Public awareness needs to be raised about this disgraceful situation. (Gibbs 1988, 159)

Most of our nation's black poor tend to live in central city ghettos. White poor tend to live in suburbs and rural settings. These residential differences may explain the disparities in delinquency and interactions with police—as well as the persistence of racism in law enforcement.

More than half the juveniles imprisoned in state institutions have a close relative already in prison. A feature article in *The New York Times* (September 13, 1992) equated doing time in prison (or juvenile facilities) for young black males to "going off to the Army" in past generations. It is stressful, yes, but so common it imparts a certain life-experience pride. "Some young brothers seem like they don't care if they go to prison," explained one inmate. "They think it's macho, that it gives them more rank out on the street." However, the police chief of New Haven, Connecticut, put the situation differently: "The mean-spirited system of justice we have in this country has perpetuated the problem" (Terry 1992).

The United States has more than 1 million people locked up— more per capita than any other industrialized nation (with South Africa in second place). In the 1980s, prison populations swelled by 130 percent. The reasons behind that huge increase include not only an increase in crimes committed, but between 1973 and 1983, forty-nine states enacted mandatory sentencing laws for drug-involved arrests. The Federal Anti-Drug Act of 1986 took most of the discretion for sentencing out of the hands of judges. As a result, the percentage of drug offenders in federal prison has risen from 34 percent in 1985 to 60 percent in 1992. Their average sentences have increased from two years to six years.

If these changes had any impact on the drug trafficking, they might be justified; but they have had no effect. What is worse, violent, dangerous offenders have had to be released early to make room for the flood of mostly nonviolent drug offenders. Federal judges and attorneys have protested this dangerous and inequitable state of law. One federal judge retired in frustration. Drug offenders are predominately young, poor males from inner cities— that is, young black males. Kingpins in the drug trade are rarely touched; squealers receive leniency. "Outrageously long sentences" are imposed on youthful offenders that provide little deterrence and turn out angry ex-cons with no capacity to find legal work ("Nightline" with Ted Koppel, "Drug Offenders in Federal

Prison," July 14, 1993). This country has socialized an entire generation to incarceration.

The so-called war on drugs may have begun as a political
response to the threat of inner-city crime, but by 1994 it has been
revealed to be an instrument of racism. Studies by the F.B.I. and the
National Institute on Drug Abuse have found that blacks make up
only about 12 percent of the nation's drug users, roughly the
proportion of blacks in the population at large. The war on drugs,
however, has focused largely on poor, urban, mostly minority
neighborhoods. "Street sellers of crack are easier to arrest than
suburban cocaine users" (Terry 1992). Of inmates in our prisons
today, about half are black or Hispanic, and over 60 percent have
not completed high school and had incomes of $10,000 or less prior
to incarceration. Nationwide, on any given day, almost one in four
of black men between the ages of twenty and twenty-nine is in
prison, on parole, or on probation.

Terry Williams, a professor at the New School for Social Research in New York, wrote about drugs and crime in *Crack House*.
He said that kids don't glorify jail, and that they are frightened of
gang rapes and other jail terrors. Joining a gang in prison becomes
necessary for survival. "But if going [to jail] is becoming a rite of
passage, it's a rite of passage by default. If there were jobs and job
training available, most of these kids who are selling drugs would
quit in a second and go to work" (cited in Terry 1992).

A young black American male has a greater chance of going to
prison than going to college. He is truly an "endangered species:"
three times more likely than his white counterpart to live in poverty; three times more likely to be killed by police; six times more
likely to be killed in the streets by other youth; five times more
likely to be arrested for robbery; and twice as likely to drop out of
school. Combining the statistics on crime, killings, and incarceration, it is understandable why people speak of the "genocide" of
young black males in this country (Gibbs 1988, Hacker 1992).

Fears and misunderstandings between the races on these issues
are exacerbated by popular stories and exaggerations in the media.
Los Angeles—home to the original Crips and Bloods—has the
most publicized gang problems. Yet other cities face worse problems—Detroit and Washington, D.C., for example. I have to stress
that 90 to 95 percent of young people in Los Angeles are not in

gangs. Most young black males do not join gangs and do not participate in criminal activities. Contrary to popular media portrayals, only a small percentage of gang members are involved in the drug trade. Officials estimate that no more than one in six or seven of Los Angeles County gang members are involved in the drug trade. For example, in one Los Angeles district in 1988, there were 96 gang-related deaths of which only seven were related to drugs (Prothrow-Stith 1991, 105).

Media interest in gangs has come and gone over recent decades. Gang participation has remained about the same. What *has* changed is that gang life has become much more dangerous.

TEACH THEM WELL

There are two reasons why this book about gangs will focus on education: First, the risks that poor urban children face turn into serious problems in their lives at very young ages—often as young as nine or ten years old. If we are to address these problems as a nation, where else but in schools do we begin to coordinate support for these nine or ten year old children in trouble? Health problems, lack of family stability, physical abuse, violent behaviors, under-achievement in school—all of these risk factors will blossom into problems with the law, dropping out of school, and unemployment if they are not addressed at a young age. From the child in trouble's point of view, it makes no sense to moralize that parents should take responsibility for such problems. Blaming parents does not solve the problems of children dropping out of school and joining gangs. The problems of troubled middle-class youth are treated in private mental health institutions; the problems of troubled poor youth are treated in jails.

A second reason to focus on education is because every gang member I have ever known, and every one I interviewed for this book, said he or she would rather be in school than in jail or in a gang. If they had a choice, they would stay in school, graduate, find a job and participate in the American dream—get married, buy a house and a car and raise a family. For too many ghetto youth, that life appears to be an impossible dream. However much gang members may have failed in the schools, the schools have failed them equally.

Consider the grim statistics: Many poor youth tend to drop out of school. *More* poor whites—about 40 percent—than poor blacks—about 30 percent—drop out of school (Gibbs 1988, 120). A student starting ninth grade in California has a three in ten chance of not graduating. Of those who do graduate, the average reading proficiency is below ninth grade level (Mecca et al. 1989). This crisis includes all races and backgrounds: California school children are 66.6 percent minority, but only 8.6 per cent black.

Almost half of American black boys (and 38 percent of black girls) begin junior high school one year or more behind the national average level of achievement (Margaret C. Simms,"Public Schools: Chance or Choice?" in *Black Enterprise*, May 1993). Various surveys have estimated that about one fifth of all black youth are unable to read beyond the fourth grade level, have dropped out of high school, and do not have either the basic skills nor the basic certificate necessary for most entry level jobs, apprenticeship programs, military service, or postsecondary education. One most pessimistic critic estimates that in Chicago schools, nearly half the children (overwhelmingly minority) who start kindergarten will exit school as "marginal illiterates" (Gibbs 1988, 6, Kozol 1991, 58).

Kahlil, an Oakland Crip whose story is in Chapter 4 said, "If somebody had cared about me, maybe things might have been a little bit different. I might be able to read a little bit better, maybe. But, nobody took any time out. I don't remember any of my teachers taking any time out. They didn't help me do anything. That's really about it."

The more positive news is that dropout rates have been declining, and average achievement for African American children has been rising at all levels. However, this brightening picture is clouded by the decline in numbers and percentages of black high school graduates able to attend college, and by the persistently high proportions of black children who are placed in lower track classes, labelled as EMR (educable mentally retarded), and suspended from schools.

Chapter 2 will address the problems for poor and minority children in schools in greater detail. Here, I simply wish to say that getting an education in schools has been a great source of hope for African Americans since the time of slavery. But, as Jonathan Kozol eloquently described in *Savage Inequalities*, that hope remains an unrealized dream in many depressed, decrepit and inadequate public urban schools. We need to begin the task of saving America's children in America's classrooms.

When I advocate that we solve the problems of inner-city children while they are in elementary school, I do not mean that such problems cannot be solved later. The resilience of these children in the face of a terrible environment is amazing. In fact, this book is about that triumph of spirit over adversity—what I call "The Hope Factor." Thousands of young people growing up in ghettos, going to substandard schools and surviving the peril of gangs have escaped the dangerous streets, gone to college, and excelled in business, education, entertainment or sports. Many of their stories appear in Chapters 3, 4 and 5.

I advocate solving these problems when children are young because they can better be addressed at a young age, they cost less to ameliorate then, and, most important, they rescue a young life from years of continued deprivation or possible death. The gang members and ex-gang members whose stories make up this book said to me, "Reach them in elementary school. Teach them then. When they're older, it's too late." However, many of the stories we report, from Westside Study Center in the 1960s to Pace School in Los Angeles today, show that it's never too late. Street youth have more capacity to change and grow than they themselves realize.

"Show them all the beauty that they have inside." The beauty inside a young child eager to learn shines through in the faces of children from all races and backgrounds. That beauty can survive boredom, abuse, sickness, loneliness, even repeated failure. In dozens of young gang members and former gang members, I saw that beauty re-emerge when they found hope, purpose, and some meaning in life through making a connection with others.

GIVE THEM A SENSE OF PRIDE

The key to rediscovering "the beauty that they have inside" is rebuilding self-esteem. The State of California decided that self-esteem was so important for the condition of people's lives that in 1986, the legislature established the "California Task Force to Promote Self-Esteem and Personal and Social Responsibility." The findings of the task force on a number of different dimensions were published in 1989 (Mecca et al).

In general, self-esteem is a result of one's experience (how people treat you) and one's inner opinion of self-worth (how you see yourself in relation to others). The psychologist Jewelle Taylor Gibbs reported that general surveys of self-esteem find little difference between black and white children and adolescents:

However, sex differences in self-esteem indicate that young black females generally report higher levels of self-esteem than young black males and this effect increases with age through young adulthood. . . . The links between low self-esteem, psychological disorder and behavioral dysfunction have been extensively documented in the social science literature. (Gibbs 1988, 237)

Whether school achievement influences self-esteem or the other way around makes little difference. Once a child repeatedly fails in school, self-esteem will plummet, and that low self-esteem then becomes the greatest barrier to further learning. Self-worth as a motivator is so strong that students will adopt a wide variety of strategies to protect self-worth and not risk failure, everything from cheating to procrastinating to not trying at all. One way to encourage students to give up such counterproductive strategies is to change the rules of the achievement "game" from a zero-sum game with a few winners and many losers to a cooperative undertaking with the goal of learning for all.

In the California task force report on self-esteem and learning, Martin V. Covington described "the need to establish and maintain feelings of worth and dignity" as among the strongest human motivators. In competitive settings with few rewards available to only a few students, most of the "losers" will slip into patterns of failure avoidance instead of seeking learning, and the least successful will demonstrate "learned helplessness" (Mecca et al. 1989, 72–111).

Cooperative learning and mastery learning shift the game from competitive to "equity paradigms"; from *what* to think to *how* to think. Such settings increase the likelihood that students will choose to work on challenging yet reasonable tasks for which success is uncertain but not impossible (Mecca et al. 1989, 72–124).

Again, there are the two dimensions to self-esteem: how we see ourselves and how others see and treat us. The ideal learning setting addresses both needs. Children (indeed, all people) need to experience success to have confidence; and more confidence creates more success. There is the external reward—teacher's praise, others' perception of excellence, or some quantifiable measure of success. The internal reward is important as well. We have to believe that what we achieved was worth doing, and that we achieved it through effort, not luck.

Self-esteem is essential for "The Hope Factor" in urban youth. In my experiences with gang members and former gang members, hope returned when a person renewed self-worth through helping someone else. "Raymond," at Pace School (in Chapter 5), said about helping handicapped children: "Most people out on the street our age feel that they have all the problems in the world. They come to this school and find out there are people worse off than them. That kind of opens your eyes. Helps you appreciate the way that you are. It kinda makes you feel needed when you work with the kids."

I call this being able to "jump-start" self-esteem. This is a fundamental human motivation. You cannot overcome educational deficiencies overnight. And it requires a lot of confidence to try hard again, especially when you have failed so many times in the past. That confidence *can* be found in doing something for someone else—and all of us have something we can do for others. For gang members, much of their motivation in joining a gang relates to enhancing self-esteem, one way or another.

The "equity paradigm" works well in most settings of human interaction. This book focuses on education because education is the instrument of "The Hope Factor" for American youth. Through equal educational opportunity, young people buy into the system which supposedly gives everyone a chance to excel, to make their contribution and to participate. If education is only defined in terms of a few winners and mostly losers, with the cards stacked against the urban poor, then the losers will be shut out from participation and prosperity and will feel they have very little stake in society.

THE HOPE FACTOR AND URBAN YOUTH

The goal of this book is to show in the stories of gang members and former gang members that positive solutions can be found to the crisis of American urban youth. This book is also my educational story. I shared similar challenges as these young black men. I was luckier and maybe more persistent. Times have not gotten easier in terms of economic opportunities for youth—especially uneducated black youth. Legalized segregation and lynchings have become relics of the past, but de facto segregation in housing and schools keeps the races almost as separated as before.

Legalized violence against black youth on the streets and in prisons, and the epidemic killings of each other by black male youth, have replaced the earlier horrors of Jim Crow. Jewelle Taylor Gibbs noted the similarities between the slave plantations of old and present-day, inner-city "welfare plantations": under slavery, black men were segregated, families were broken up, education was forbidden, life-expectancy was bleak. "Urban ghettos are rapidly becoming 'welfare plantations,' cut off from vital urban centers of culture and commerce by inadequate transportation, lack of an economic base, and lack of political power" (Gibbs 1988, 27).

"The Hope Factor" relates to the American Dream of material prosperity—that any one can make it. It is essential for the citizens' faith in a democracy. But it goes beyond materialism. From the grim facts presented in this chapter, it is clear that poor black youth cannot survive or become part of mainstream American society without economic improvement. But the descendants of slaves in this country were always seeking more than material gain. African American spiritual and aesthetic gifts, from Gospel and Jazz to break dancing and slam dunking, have transformed this culture.

This country has always stood for more than material prosperity. If the most important value in a society is material wealth, then many people will always be angry and envious. The media will forever portray the next unattainable level of luxury. Some social critics say we have reached this selfish, negative and dangerous state already.

In *The End of Equality*, Mickey Kaus argues that "liberals have been distracted by an unnecessary and unrewarding obsession with the very thing they should be trying to render less significant, namely money." Today's social inequality also derives from the breakdown of public institutions such as public schools, playgrounds and parks, and the common draft for military service, which used to offer equal dignity to people from many different backgrounds. Basic human rights in education, health care and political power are as essential to democracy as fair and just economic rewards.

"The Hope Factor," then, is about more than getting out of the lower class. All Americans need "The Hope Factor." It is also about finding a reason for living. Helping others—cooperation— holds the key to a meaningful existence. Our whole global village needs to pull together to educate the children of the world. There are practical reasons to do so—better educated people can do useful work and solve problems, and they are less likely to tear each other apart in wars. And there are moral, spiritual reasons to do so.

Traditionally, African Americans have loved their own and others' children in extended families and close-knit communities. Black women cared for the white children of the slave owners and, later, of the upper classes. Today's children need to see cooperation as an alternative to competition; success in the place of failure; pride instead of humiliation; empathy instead of anger; knowledge in place of confusion; and empowerment overcoming frustration.

MY PERSONAL JOURNEY

My educational experience paralleled the dramatic changes in this country from legalized racial segregation, to the Civil Rights Movement, to the high hopes and progress of the 1960s and 1970s for African Americans, to the backlash and economic stagnation of the 1980s for all Americans, to the crisis today of the urban black male "underclass" who are nonparticipants in terms of mainstream jobs and education, and who are on the brink of genocide.

To my own educational experience as it intertwined with national events and trends, I applied my belief in "The Hope Factor." I knew I would always be black; but I was determined that I would not always be poor: I would get an education, despite the obstacles. I believed that education pointed the way up and out of the box a black male in America was born into.

Two factors made the difference for me in terms of my chances for success: the influence and support of my parents, and the influence of my peers in junior and senior high school in San Diego, California. Our club, "The Lucky 13," had high ambitions. We turned our energies towards sports and leadership and positive outlets. We were "luckier" than other youth who turned in the opposite direction. The times were propitious, and every one of us did well, either through education, the military, or job success. On many dimensions, we were not very different from the young Crips or Bloods in Los Angeles today. But we had different options, and we made different choices.

In the process of raising a large family and also helping out an extended family, my parents taught me the virtues of hard work, self-respect and empathy. From my mother I derived a love for children. Not only was she always taking care of her own children, she was taking care of others' children too, even while working full-time. I cannot enter a classroom, whatever the race or background of the children, without hurting with them when I see the curtailment of their opportunities and the diminishing of their dreams.

My parents were originally from the deep South in northeast Louisiana. My father was unusual in the community. From him I inherited pride and a bent for leadership. My father was mixed race: Native American, black and white. So, as my family would say, "He hadn't learned to be a slave." In the South in those times, such a community leader would be called a "Crazy Nigger" because he stood up to intimidation and refused to "shuffle." For example, he interfered to stop one of the customary whippings called "going on the log" that were administered when a sharecropper did not meet his production quota. When the Ku Klux Klan came to visit, the story goes that he recognized his prominent neighbors beneath their white sheets by their shoes and confronted them by name: "You, Henry. You better get on out of here."

My father was a landowner when most blacks were sharecroppers. My family was never hungry. My father had a big horse and two guns. He had to leave the state on that horse and a spare after one too many run-ins with the Ku Klux Klan and the sheriff.

My mother followed my father to California months later, when it was safe, with my older brother and sister. She had to tell white people she was going to visit relatives in Texas. Until El Paso, where the Jim Crow laws ended, she had to ride in the front of the train where the cinders blew in on you.

I was born later on the California-Mexico border, near El Centro where we eventually owned a farm. When my mother would return to Louisiana to visit relatives, she would not take us younger children along. She claimed that since growing up in California, we were a menace to ourselves in the South because "We didn't know how to act." (She did not offer her opinion on the fact that apparently my father didn't know how to act either.)

READING THIS BOOK

This book is addressed to educators and, especially, to young, beginning teachers who will most likely find their first jobs in America's cities in multicultural classrooms. Many of the children in those classrooms will be poor; most will be from minorities; many will be immigrants or children of immigrants. At a time in history when we need to marshal all our skills and knowledge to support cultural differences and combat racism, we have been sliding backwards. In the 1950s, black people could not ride in the front of a bus; in the 1960s, black men were still lynched in the South; today, this society is growing and changing, but ignorance and hate still abound. What is intelligence? I would maintain that a crucial part of intelligence is understanding other people and being able to care about the fate of all children.

To know and love others, you also have to know and love yourself. That is why I have not left my personal story out of the story of endangered urban youth. One educator wrote the following about good teaching: "If it is important to get students inside a subject, it is equally important to get the subject inside the students. . . . When we ignore autobiography, we create educated monsters who know much about the world's external workings but little about their inner selves" (Palmer 1990).

Becoming educated is more than learning about external realities. It is growing internally as well. One of my teaching colleagues asked me how to respond to what seemed to him shocking bigotry from students in his teacher education class. Several students had said, "Different people want to keep separate and maybe they should. You shouldn't have blacks and whites getting married, because their children don't know where they fit in."

To my colleague I replied, "How could these students not be biased?" They have not been exposed to anything else. This society has become more racist in all of its communications in recent years. Students, especially future teachers, need to be exposed to people from other backgrounds. Although that is just the beginning, most teacher education schools fail to meet even that fundamental need.

Teachers today are totally unprepared for interacting with children from poor and minority backgrounds. Thrown into the challenge of urban classrooms, they see the children as less than human. They have to become knowledgeable and learn more about others and about themselves. Otherwise, they remain bigoted by default. White middle-class youth in general have the same symptoms of diminished hope as black street youth: They are frightened about the future and fearful of the motives of others. Like the gang members we interviewed, before they can reach out to others, they have to learn to love and accept themselves.

The heart of this book is stories told by black youth, particularly males in or formerly in gangs. There is hope in their stories in the midst of terrible conditions. Even the hardest gang member longs for his unrealized education. With a few exceptions (and the same can be said about any urban police force), these are not hardened criminals or killers. They want the same things that most American youth want—recognition, success, love. But if the killing and tragic waste of lives continues, I am afraid that more gang-affiliated youth will retreat into a numb shell of indifference to their own life and that of others.

Our futures are intertwined.

Chapter 2, "Education and Black Youth" reviews the major urban educational issues with their historical settings. My own educational experiences are woven into each section. Chapter 3, "Westside Stories," tells about the community action agency I founded in the 1960s, during the early years of my educational work. Pasadena, California, was a microcosm of larger cities in the problems faced by street youth. From Westside came my philosophy of "The Hope Factor."

In Chapter 4, I return to the Los Angeles area twenty-seven years later and interview gang members and former gang members. My focus is education: what they experienced in schools, how and why they joined gangs, and their hopes for the future. Pace School in Los Angeles County, in Chapter 5, provides a present-day example of "The Hope Factor" in action for youthful ex-gang members.

In Chapter 6, I explore "Institutional Racism and Renewal." Some examples are historical, such as, the American Military, and some are case studies from my educational work at the University of Massachusetts at Amherst, such as the Boston Secondary Schools Project. Chapter 7 revisits the major themes of the book with positive examples and suggestions for improving urban education. It proposes "A National Agenda to Save Urban Youth" with the message, "It's not easy, but we know enough."

The motto we chose for Westside Study Center, "Time Is Running Out," takes on new urgency today in light of the endangered future of our youth. This book is needed right now, not only for black youth, but for white youth and everyone else. The suicide rate of all teenagers is higher than it has ever been in the history of America. Most Americans say they do not expect their lives to get much better in the near future. One in five children in young married families, of all races and backgrounds, is now poor. Fears of crime have driven people into private, protected enclaves with gates, locks and security guards. It does not take much imagination in some parts of urban America to think you are in a third world country ruled by drug lords and corrupt private armies. Beverly Hills and South Central L.A. could be Medellin, Columbia, or Rio de Janeiro, Brazil. We can do better. We must offer something better to our children.

NOTE

1. These figures, commonly reported by media, change slightly each year and are annually updated by the Children's Defense Fund and other reports, based on national statistical sources such as the Census and the Bureau of Labor Statistics.

chapter two

Education and Black Youth

❏ ❏ ❏

In the late 1970s, while a faculty member in urban education at the University of Massachusetts, Amherst, I served as a Title I consultant. One of my responsibilities was to visit schools to see how federal funds to supplement education for poor children were spent. I went to visit an elementary school of mostly poor and minority children in an old city on the coast of New England. One third grade classroom had an "innovative" way to deal with disruptive children. Using Title I funds, the teachers had created what they called the "time-out lab" out of a former coat closet attached to the classroom. In this tiny room with one small window, a child who was disruptive would be isolated. When I saw that set up, I was very disturbed. All that was missing in this training for jail was the bucket in the corner!

This was only third grade! I observed one little black boy when he was let out (furloughed) to return to the class. When the teacher was not looking, three kids would hit him until he hit back, and then he would be in trouble again. He was a really smart little boy. I asked him how long they left him in the "time-out lab." He said, "Can I tell you? Two hours sometimes." It really upset me that teachers would think this was all right. If "the human touch" is racist and cruel like that, I'd rather the child interact with only a computer. That child was not a really troublesome student. The teacher did not notice the other students picking on him. I do not want to disparage teachers either, but this example of training a child for a life in jail was appalling.

I experienced a similarly discouraging visit to a Massachusetts mill town of predominantly poor and lower-class white children. A doctoral student of mine who would eventually become super-intendent of that school district took me to visit a working class school. The children were all poor and white. The school was neat and clean and the children were well-behaved. However, the kin-dergarten pre-tested all the children and assigned them to tracks before they had even made it to first grade. The principal was pleasant enough, but not very imaginative. Some of these kids had already flunked life before they started! Only a chosen group was going to get a good education. The nice school with its nice teachers was just awful. I met a sixth grader they had labelled as retarded. She was helping out by taking care of the kindergarten. She did not appear retarded to me. No other school in the system had those pre-kindergarten tests. However, this was a poor community, and the parents did not expect anything more for their children's education.

The children I observed in those two schools should be gradu-ating from high school today, if they made it that far. Those two anecdotes show that racism, classism and low expectations come in all colors in schools. We need "The Hope Factor" for all those children, even if the parents and teachers do not hope for anything more.

In this chapter, we will survey the most important issues in education for poor and minority children in American schools. I want to emphasize that the opportunities we want to develop for a meaningful life through education should be there for all chil-dren, regardless of race, religion, sex or economic background.

EDUCATION AND EQUALITY

When I was a boy in school, like many African Americans, I saw education as the path to success and partaking in the American Dream. This belief in equal opportunity underlies our nation's political and moral debate over the role of public education. It was not always so. During the second half of the Eighteenth century, the earliest free public high schools were designed to serve only a minority of youth who showed unusual intellectual or religious talent and whose families could forego their labor.

Charles Eliot, President of Harvard University, chaired the first National Education Association committee on secondary education for standardizing curricula in 1892. He suggested that all high school students be exposed to a rigorous college preparation curriculum, whether or not they were college-bound, noting that educators tended to underestimate students' capabilities. Unfortunately, that egalitarian position was swamped by the events that followed.

After the turn of the century, immigrants poured into American cities at the rate of nearly a million a year—15 million by 1924. They were predominantly Southern European and less than welcomed by Anglo-European Americans. Public school enrollments increased by over 700 percent. By 1909, 58 percent of students in thirty-seven of the largest cities were of foreign-born parentage (Oakes 1985).

(This level of immigration pressure and the Tower of Babel of languages in schools was not duplicated until the late 1970s and 1980s when approximately 13 million immigrated, coming mostly from Asia, Mexico, the Caribbean and South America. Indeed, because of the dramatic changes in the past decade, demographers are challenged to categorize groups. Consider for example, the variety of minorities of Spanish-speaking heritage: Does "Hispanic" or "Latino" include wealthy, white Cubans as well as rural, black Puerto Ricans—or Mexicans or Salvadorans? Some Asian immigrant groups academically outperform everyone, while others suffer as much discrimination and poverty as inner city black Americans. Are they all "minorities"?)

By the 1920s, the nineteenth-century ideal of common learning to build a cohesive nation was gone. Gone, too, was Eliot's idea of a challenging curriculum for all secondary students. Social Darwinists ("survival of the human fittest") advocated different kinds of education for different economic needs. Americanization in public schools now meant shaping those "undisciplined" and "unclean" Southern European hordes into hard-working, tidy workers who respected WASP (white-Anglo-Saxon-Protestant) values. At the same time, a fascination with the new industrial efficiencies, "scientific management," was applied to schools as well as to large businesses. Schools stepped into the role of sorting students for various occupations by providing them with differentiated training and skills, a role in the industrial order they continue to this day.

Vocational education came into being, and junior high schools were established in order to start the sorting process early (by age twelve). While it seemed to some that this tracking of youngsters based mostly on their parental heritage was "un-American" or antidemocratic, the discovery of I.Q. testing during World War I made such sorting "scientific" and more palatable. The fact that the first I.Q. tests labelled about 80 percent of the immigrants feeble-minded did not deter the testing pioneers (Oakes 1985).

African American educational history followed a different course. In the antebellum South, it was illegal to educate slaves. This law was often broken, especially in the case of the master's own "mulatto" offspring. In the North, schools for freemen were established, and some former slaves attended colleges (which, in the early 1800s, were predominantly seminaries). While Quakers and other abolitionists pioneered equal education for all races, for women as well as men, Southern and border states resisted free Negro equality. In 1847, Missouri State law made it illegal to provide schooling for free blacks or mulattos.

After the Civil War, the powerful lure of education within the African American community was demonstrated: By 1890, one third of black children under age 21 were enrolled in schools. That proportion reached 45 percent by 1910, less than two generations after slavery (Billingsley 1992). After the liberation of slaves in the Civil War and the racist backlash following Reconstruction, the World War I era witnessed a tremendous exodus of African Americans to jobs and the relatively less overt segregation in industrial cities of the North, Midwest and far West. During each decade, from 1920 to 1960, more than ten percent of the black population left the South.

Following the devastating unemployment of the Great Depression of the 1930s (whites were almost 25 percent unemployed, and blacks as much as 80 percent), World War II brought new civilian job opportunities and participation in the armed forces for African

Americans. The Civil Rights Movement of the 1950s and 1960s built on those gains and renewed hopes for better jobs and education.

In 1954, the Supreme Court ruled that separate, even if "equal," schools in the South were unconstitutional because by their very existence they were prejudicial and implied inferiority. Other key Civil Rights strategies focused on securing voting rights and de-segregating public accommodations and transportation. In education, the goal shifted to integrating schools, both in the South and the North. The factory model of schools efficiently preparing students to play their preordained roles in life was brought into question. Because residential segregation proved resistant to change, the strategy of busing to achieve racial balance in schools was adopted.

The hope that school integration would provide equal opportunity for all Americans ran smack into the combined forces of racism and fundamental economic and demographic changes. As Andrew Billingsley and other sociologists have noted, "blacks lost ground in upward mobility in public schools after the Supreme Court decision outlawing segregation in 1954" (Billingsley 1992, 192).

From the 1950s, onward, while poor Americans and immigrants continued to settle in inner cities to look for jobs, middle-class Americans and an ever-increasing proportion of work opportunities were moving out to suburbs, away from the crowding, decay, high taxes and crime of central cities. The federally subsidized interstate highway system replaced rail lines in transportation importance. Cars carried commuters to work from homes in the suburbs. Trucks relayed products from point to point for businesses that to this day continue to move away from central cities.

What appeared on the surface to be a positive economic and social program for the cities—"urban renewal"—often became in fact a program of "urban removal." Old, multi-family, decaying ghetto housing was torn down. On those locations were built new highways to serve suburban commuters, better housing that was unaffordable to the poor, or new middle-class shopping complexes. The displaced families and poor individuals had no place to go. High-rise public housing built to accommodate some of those displaced usually turned into violent, decaying, high-rise ghettos, worse than the old neighborhoods that had been torn down.

The post-World War II prosperity won by high-paying blue collar jobs eroded after 1970 as the economy evolved from the manufacturing age to the age of information—from an industrial to a post-industrial society. Heavy manufacturing jobs moved overseas, replaced by high-tech and lighter industry, health and human services, and advanced research enterprises that did not rely on central city locations. In the U.S. 1990 census, the suburban population outstripped the central cities population for the first time.

The story of Boston is illustrative of what happened in older American cities in the aftermath of the Civil Rights Movement. Federal mandates to integrate Boston schools through busing in the late 1970s met violent resistance from traditional white ethnic enclaves. Racist fear mixed with legitimate complaints about losing control over traditional community schools. The outcome was that by 1990, Boston, with a black population of 25.6 percent, had public schools that were more than 75 percent minority. White families had moved out or transferred their children to private and parochial schools. (For an outstanding ethnographic account, see Anthony Lukas, *Common Ground.*)

Other cities, small and large—such as Berkeley and San Jose, California, Seattle, Washington, Cambridge, Massachusetts, and even New York City—were more successful in achieving some improved racial balance in their schools. However, with more open housing and job opportunities emerging following the civil rights reforms of the 1960s, many middle- and upper-class African Americans departed central cities for the suburbs, increasing further the racial and economic isolation of poor and minority ghetto residents (Wilson 1987).

Even as economic and social trends in central cities were creating environments less equitable for poor and minority children in schools, public and political rhetoric moved away from Social Darwinist determinism. Political leaders and educators proclaimed the egalitarian role of education in giving every American child the opportunity to fulfill his potential and to move up in the economic lattice through merit. This philosophy certainly underlay the Civil Rights Movement, President Johnson's War on Poverty, and the discourse of educators and bureaucrats from the 1960s on.

In April 1983, the National Commission on Excellence in Education, appointed by Secretary of Education Terrell Bell, released *A Nation At Risk*. The main thrust of the report was the decline of educational achievement in America at all levels and in all arenas. Despite the conservative tone of those early years of the Reagan administration, this commission reiterated as shared American values the fundamental arguments in favor of equality in education: the economic argument, the moral argument, and the political argument.

The *economic* argument simply stated that an educated work force is a competitive work force. "If only to keep and improve on the slim competitive edge we still retain in world markets, we must dedicate ourselves to the reform of our educational system for the benefit of all—old and young alike, affluent and poor, majority and minority. Learning is the indispensable investment required for success in the 'information age' we are entering" (AASA 1983, 3).

On a global level, economists such as Robert Reich have predicted that the world market trend to richly reward well-educated "symbolic analysts," such as knowledge engineers software developers scientific researchers, medical specialists, etc., and to pay lower wages for unskilled labor (increasingly concentrated in third world countries) will surely increase in the future (Reich 1991).

Underlining the economic argument for educational equality was the fact that, when Social Security was enacted in the 1930s, eleven workers contributed to the support of each retired worker. By 2050, that ratio would drop to less than three workers for every retiree. Poorly educated and unemployed workers would not be able to contribute to a secure retirement, a potentially explosive issue when the majority of retirees will be white and the majority of workers nonwhite.

The *moral* argument for educational equality is simply that it is "right." The Excellence Commission stated:

The intellectual, moral, and spiritual strengths of our people . . . knit together the very fabric of our society. The people of the United States need to know that individuals in our society who do not possess the levels of skill, literacy, and training essential to this new era will be effectively disenfranchised, not simply from the material rewards that accompany competent performance, but also from the chance to participate fully in our national life. (AASA 1983, 3)

Finally, in this 1983 historic study of American education, we came full circle to the *political* arguments for equality of education, similar to those expressed 100 years ago by Charles Eliot: "A high level of shared education is essential to a free, democratic society and to the fostering of a common culture, especially in a country that prides itself on pluralism and individual freedom" (AASA 1983, 3).

That most Americans shared the beliefs expressed in the Excellence Report was supported by a Gallup Poll of "The Public's Attitudes Toward the Public Schools": "Americans are steadfast in their belief that education is the major foundation for the future strength of this country." They even considered education more important than developing the best industrial system or the strongest military force. They also felt that education is "extremely important" to one's future success, and that public education should be the top priority for additional federal funds. (AASA 1983).

A subsequent Gallup Poll, in 1989, showed that "A convincing majority of the public (83 percent) believes that more should be done to improve the quality of the public schools in poorer states and communities. Of this 83 percent, 62 percent (over half of all respondents) said they would be willing to pay more taxes for that purpose."

RACE AND CLASS

I started elementary school in El Centro, California, in a segregated school. Most black and Mexican families lived on one side of the railroad tracks; whites lived on the other. Each sub-community had its own schools. If there were any white children living on our side of the tracks, the school bus came to pick them up and transport them to the white school. My nephew was the first in our family to go to the integrated high school, years later, across the tracks.

El Centro was the county seat for the Imperial Valley. It was predominantly agricultural. The black teachers of higher status and the principal lived just across the tracks. Not everyone in the black community was necessarily eager to give up segregated schools. If any college-educated family member or friend from the big cities like San Diego or Los Angeles could not find a teaching job, they could always come back to El Centro and work for the school system.

However, the black schools had only hand-me-down books and curriculum—whatever was no longer wanted at the white schools. When I moved to San Diego in third grade, I went from that tiny rural segregated school to large, integrated schools. They were not wealthy schools, and you had to be ready to fight, but they presented a much larger world to me. I began my own experience in urban education in America.

A broader perspective on the critical issues of race and class in American schooling is a necessary backdrop to the individual stories told in this book. That broader picture should encompass an overview of race and class in American education, zoom in to the roles of race and class within individual schools (especially tracking), and then explore individual responses to racism or lowered expectations within the classroom. The rest of this chapter will present those layers of perspective on race and class, from a bird's-eye view to individual experiences.

The majority white American public "discovered" urban education as a problem in the 1950s and 1960s through movies like *Blackboard Jungle*, books like *Up the Down Staircase* and Jonathan Kozol's *Death at an Early Age*. The latter especially focused sympathies and attention on racism, punitive tracking, violence and run-down conditions in urban schools.

When social scientists and educational researchers turned their attention to urban education, they took a quantitative view, gathering and analyzing statistics to support generalizations. The massive, federally-funded *Coleman Report* of 1966 unearthed the conclusion that the single greatest factor which correlated with student achievement in schools was the socioeconomic status of the student's parents. The next greatest factor was the socioeconomic status of the other students in the classroom. The disturbing conclusion that perhaps schools *don't* make much difference was followed by the more disturbing conclusions of Christopher Jencks, in *Inequality*, that schools perhaps *can't* make much difference. His research claimed that not all of the gap between average white and black academic achievement could be attributed to environment, but might also depend on hereditary differences.

Neither teachers nor parents accepted findings that contradicted their common sense and experience: They knew that good teachers and good teaching make a big difference in students' educational achievement, and that all races have equal capacities to learn. Both the scientific validity and the motivation behind Jencks' and others' (Shockley, Herrnstein, Eysenck, Seligman) research have been discredited. Furthermore, idle speculation over small statistical differences in innate abilities, whether between boys and girls or between blacks and whites, had no practical application in the classroom. What could hypothetical average differences in *group* achievements mean or matter when a classroom teacher has to assess the progress of an individual student?

Finally, no one would dispute that all healthy children from any racial or economic background are surely capable of mastering basic skills and a fundamental level of language and mathematic literacy—levels which too many urban schools fail to achieve. Public Law 94–142, passed by Congress in 1965, recognizes this truism and calls for "mainstreaming" of almost all students through individual educational planning.

While these debates raged in academic and political circles, conditions in inner-city schools got worse. In their 1987 analysis, *The Color Line and the Quality of Life*, Farley and Allen summarized the status of the American Dream twenty years after the Watts uprising and the *Kerner Commission Report* on its causes. In general, they said, most immigrant groups had claimed great progress after several generations; and, despite perceptions, black Americans also made great progress in the previous three generations. "But the counterpoint to that success is the disproportionate number of black Americans mired in poverty." Furthermore, "although blacks are approaching whites in the quantity of education (years of schooling), they in fact continue to be far behind in quality of education (revealed in standardized test scores)" (Farley and Allen 1987, 4, 204).

Into this body of research, which seemed devoid of common sense, came the "school effectiveness movement" and its attendant research, led by the late African American educational scholar, Ronald Edmonds. He patiently explored those factors that characterized successful inner-city schools serving predominantly minority students. In 1981, Herman E. Behling, Jr. wrote, "Many people in education who have not been reading recent research believe we do not know what good schools and classrooms are, and other people outside education believe that learning is controlled by factors over which educators have no control. Both of these groups are in error" ("What Recent Research Says About Effective Schools and Effective Classrooms," unpublished research report 1981, i). Later, in 1985, Ross Zenchykov reported at a national conference hosted by the Institute for Responsive Education (Mott Foundation), that school effectiveness research "provided data that resurrected the possibility of the American Dream of the common school as a vehicle for democracy. It did so by discovering that despite the obvious benefits of [economic] class, some schools do make a difference" ("A Citizen's Notebook for Effective Schools," 1985, 14).

As Edmonds concluded, effective schools share strong administrative leadership, especially in instructional matters, a school climate conducive to learning, school-wide emphasis on basic skills instruction, high teacher expectations, and a system for monitoring and assessing tied to instructional objectives. Effective classroom instruction exhibits extensive time on academic tasks, highly structured question sessions with a high rate of correct answers, immediate academic feedback, both whole class and small group instruction, and monitoring of performance during recitation (Edmonds 1979).

A second layer of related research, to which we will return in later chapters, explored how some inner-city schools, despite difficult odds, became effective schools and how they stayed that way.

A common sense corollary to the importance of good teaching is that money spent on schools really does matter. Attractive and well-supplied schools with well-compensated staff can create islands of hope in areas of poverty, crime and isolation. Jonathan Kozol revisited urban public schools and reported in *Savage Inequalities* that the disparities he saw between impoverished urban schools and their suburban counterparts were worse in 1992 than he had observed twenty-five years before (Kozol 1991).

Because almost half the financing of public schools comes from local property taxes, per pupil expenditures are held hostage to the value of local real estate. A poor community may tax itself twice as much per $1,000 valuation and still collect only half as much per pupil as a wealthy community right next door. Students from homes already below the poverty line experience the additional handicap of going to underfunded schools. After researching inequities in Baltimore schools, Robert Slavin of Johns Hopkins said, "No industrialized countries give the poorest children the least, except the U.S. and South Africa, perhaps for the same reason" (Winerip 1993, 17).

Contrary to popular belief, the federal government's contribution to public schools is tiny—5.6 percent in 1990, down from 9.16 percent in 1980 (Margaret C. Simms, "Public Schools: Chance or Choice" Joint Center of Political and Economic Studies, Washington, D.C., in *Black Enterprise*, May 1993). The states make up about 47 percent of the funding for public schools, and that contribution has declined somewhat in recent years as well. Disparities among states are great.

Money can't buy you love, but being poor can put quite a strain on a marriage. Money can't buy you wisdom, but it certainly is one important ingredient in a quality education. At this point in time, legal and legislative challenges are taking place in many states with the goal of equalizing such gross disparities in local financial educational resources. In 1993, Michigan became the second state (after Hawaii) to discontinue the local property tax to finance schools.

Even in more affluent and successful school districts, the practice of tracking or "ability grouping" rations access to high quality instruction for poor and minority students. When I first moved to San Diego and attended integrated schools, I knew that as a black male, my greatest danger was being sent to the lowest track—being exiled to "the dumb room." Once there I would never get out. Today, in our liberal university community of Amherst, Massachusetts, there is tremendous resistance to abandoning tracking in the local high school, despite a civil rights suit filed by the NAACP.

Jeannie Oakes has written two books on tracking that review decades of research and effectively discount all claims to the efficacy of tracking, except that it sometimes makes instruction easier for the teacher. The first myth that has been effectively discredited is that there are only one or two kinds of intelligence and that they can be measured objectively by I.Q. tests. (Tests usually provide the "objective" rationale for homogeneous grouping.) Not only is human intelligence far more complex—Howard Gardner proposed at least seven different kinds of intelligences—but I.Q. tests are only useful as narrow academic predictors and contain insidious cultural biases (Gardner 1985; Oakes 1985).

Achievement tests, of course, do differentiate what some people know and others do not know; but teachers, parents and students alike quickly forget that they are not tests of what everybody does or should know. By design, they only include items that, on the whole, can discriminate levels of achievement, that is, sort out winners and losers. For instructional purposes, diagnostic tests which measure mastery are more useful.

Tracking (homogeneous grouping) has not been shown to improve outcomes for the high-track students. Heterogeneous grouping does not hinder the outcomes for any level. Tracking *has* been shown to have negative effects on average-track and, especially, on low-track students. They experience lower expectations, a watered-down curriculum and lowered self-esteem. In sum, reasons for tracking have been revealed as fallacious, but the practice continues unabated. Why? "In fact, tracking practices begin in first grade, and the ability groups to which individual students are assigned are fixed by third grade" (Gibbs 1988, 77). We will review successful structural and curricular alternatives to tracking in Chapter 7.

The overall progress but continuing plight of poor and minority students in urban schools seems to reflect the worsening socioeconomic trends we surveyed in the previous section. For all black American students in recent decades, high school graduation rates have improved and achievement scores have improved, including SATs. But the educational environment in many inner-city schools has remained destructive: a disproportionate number of black students are in lower academic tracks, lower-status vocational programs and EMR classes (73 percent of "behavior disabled" are young black males, according to Prothrow-Stith 1991, 164). A very large proportion of suspensions are of black youth, especially males. Finally, the number and proportion of African American youth attending college have declined since 1978, surely a disturbing economic indicator since more black youth have graduated from high school.

The real problem is poverty. A 1985 study of high school dropout rates for youth from *poor* families showed that 31.6 percent of black youth and a *higher* 39.6 percent of white youth from such backgrounds did not finish high school (Gibbs 1988, 120). We do not need to wait for research to tell us the relative weight of race versus the relative weight of poverty in limiting educational opportunities before we do something about improving the schools in which both seem to matter so much.

ELEMENTARY SCHOOL: THE CONFRONTATION POINT

We moved to San Diego after my father died and I entered third grade in Logan Elementary. We lived in an area with lower- and working-class whites, blacks and Mexicans. There were plenty of good government jobs building ships and airplanes, after World War II. I remember the camouflage nets and fake buildings for decoys remaining all around the city.

In the school there were two kinds of "kick out" classes—or "special needs" classes. One room still had course work but had only one teacher with forty students from three different grades. That meant you had no chance to learn anything. I already knew better than to ever get caught in that. The other was just a "keep busy" room where the students cooked, made model airplanes, and were basically kept occupied. Two of my best friends were in that class. Students were put in that class because the teachers wanted to get rid of them. In those days, teachers could just say where you had to go. So you learned the system really well if you were black, and you learned never to trust teachers, especially white teachers. I was always joining something like Junior Traffic Patrol to survive in a positive domain. My earliest bad memory in school was being made to sit under my teacher's desk on the floor as punishment for asking too many questions!

After my mother remarried, we moved to East San Diego, still keeping our house in San Diego and renting it out. This was a more white residential area, and I was the only one out of a handful of black students not in the special needs class. I was about to be assigned there, but that special needs teacher was "special," and she said, "No, he doesn't need to be in here." She told me to come by anytime I needed help with my homework.

I needed plenty of help, but I was careful not to show it. I was originally left-handed, and my first teachers made me change to my right hand. That probably did not improve a tendency to reverse letters and numbers. I missed almost a year of school because of asthma. My mother would send me back to El Centro to relatives when I was really sick. The desert air would help. I do not remember any elementary teachers helping me learn. No one ever mentioned that I was not speaking "standard" English. Somehow, I kept my self-esteem and secret ambitions. Most black boys by the third or fourth grade have lost both.

I call this "the confrontation point," because at about third or fourth grade, when schools begin national achievement testing and have established their tracks, poor children—especially black boys—begin to get the message about their place in society. Too many of them have not been taught to read well, and they have not assimilated successfully into the school culture. They are no longer little and cute, and the teachers' dislike of them and disdain for their abilities show through. Even when their early achievement is up to the level of other students, after fourth grade they fall farther and farther behind, usually entering junior high school one or two full grades behind.

The educational problems for inner-city black boys in the first three grades occur on many levels. Sometimes teachers express prejudice against them. Sometimes the minority students just get ignored, and difficulties with reading go unremediated. Sometimes black as well as white teachers convey prejudices against poorer children who are not as well-dressed, who are darker, taller, or less attractive than other children in the class. Studies have documented how kindergarten teachers tracked children by status based on physical appearance. The children themselves become accomplices in class and intelligence sorting. They see themselves and others as inferior. Gouldner did a longitudinal study of kindergarten through second grade documenting those stereotyping behaviors as "Teachers' Pets, Troublemakers and Nobodies" (Payne 1984, 107–110).

Of course these problems happen to boys—and girls as well—from many backgrounds in public schools. However, because more black boys are poor and because of racism, their problems are compounded. Some young boys react to their failures in schools with defiance. They feel frustration and anger that they turn on themselves or on others. The following reminiscence, written by "Jake," a severely dyslexic, white male prisoner in a Massachusetts prison tells a familiar story of elementary school "in the trenches." He was fortunate that one teacher gave him at least one good year of school:

I was the kind of kid that just didn't care about school or very much else. In the years that preceded I'd go very reluctantly to that first day of school and study the latest enemy. See if the teacher would be easy or hard as far as putting up with my dysfunctional attitudes.

I can see what they saw when they looked back at the enemy. My nose had been broken many times as a child and left me a chronic mouth breather. From this my teeth grew in spaced out and crooked. This apparent physically moronic look was even more complicated by what would many years later be diagnosed as dyslexia.

So every year I'd assume my defensive position and dig in for another year of trench warfare. Me against the system in a never ending barrage of "he's bright but he just doesn't try" or "perpetual day dreamer" as their explanations for their inability to communicate with me. The effects of this situation lead to a lot of frustration that ended in a don't give a shit attitude.

[In sixth grade]Enter Mrs. Sweet, a woman who would not hear of the fact that she could not reach any student. She would not feel her own self-worth if she could not touch any child which was left in her care. From the time she'd arrive in the morning in that brand new cream colored Buick and all through those long school days she would never lose her composure or cool.

So when we collided on that first day we both knew that this could be a very long and tenuous battle for us both. She did not sit in the front of the class like the other teachers but off to the right and back of the direction in which we faced. My seat was just ahead of her large hardwood desk so that she was just over my right shoulder. It occurs to me now that it was a great tactical ploy.

When she lectured she would come around to the front of the class and stand in front of those endless green chalk boards. This school was old even then with its eighteen foot ceilings and huge class rooms. When she would start to explain the mechanics of written English to a bunch of sixth graders most of us were bored to distraction.

I was especially bored for I had no grasp of the written word for the problems of such a disease are many and far reaching. In the prior grades

I would be called on to "read" and when ever this happened I'd stutter as my classmates would slowly recline in their chairs and begin to grin. So I'd start and grins would inevitably go to all out laughter.

The things that I saw on that page were as real as the print but they were not the same. In transposing words, whole sentences, and at my creative best entire paragraphs all that could be concluded was that I was completely illiterate. Math class became even more absurd. This inevitably lead to total frustration and an absolute indifference toward school and teachers.

Well Mrs. Sweet would have no part of it and was bound and determined that I would learn or know why. The control she held over the class was very subliminal and quite contrived, the way I see it now. If anyone got rambunctious or edgy she gave off a look and aura that would single out the particular individual. That look was more than effective to quell even a prison riot.

Yet somehow as she wrote all of these sentences on those green boards, and began to dissect them with lines that ran in varying directions, depending as to whether they were modifiers or dangling participles, all of this written stuff started to make sense even to an illiterate like me.

I recall now that she never called on me to read but would ask me to explain the dynamics of English and lo and behold the grasp I held was iron fisted and true. It dawned on me then that I was not an utter and complete idiot. It felt good, very good! I still could not read for four more years but the mechanics that she taught me have stayed with me all these years. But even more was that I did have a brain, which in spite of my dysfunctional problem, could be trained to deal with it and most any of life's other problems.

"Jake" is still dealing with life's problems from within jail. His story of Mrs. Sweet reminds us of the sometimes heroic teachers who can help students overcome years of neglect or abuse. The two anecdotes from schools at the beginning of this chapter illustrated that the groundwork for the confrontation point is laid in many different schools, for whites and blacks, boys and girls alike. But when the confrontation point is passed, far too many of the victims of damaged self-esteem are nine and ten year old black boys. According to a Gerald Levy study, four fifths of students in ghetto schools discover they are "dumb" by the fourth grade (Payne 1984, 118).

Children's Television Workshop, the producers of *Sesame Street* for educational television, conducted studies on the learning gains of four and five year olds who watch the show. This was probably the only study of learning in settings mostly free of racial and class biases. The results were very straightforward: regardless of race or economic class, children who watched the show for more hours learned more of its lessons (Peelle, C. "Where Children Learn," Ed.D. diss., University of Massachusetts, Amherst, 1972). Can we someday teach elementary school as joyfully, positively, and free of racial or class prejudice as *Sesame Street* does?

JUNIOR HIGH/MIDDLE SCHOOL: JAILS AND TURNING POINTS

I began my junior high school years in East San Diego, at the predominantly white Woodrow Wilson School. When my step-father died, we moved back to San Diego, but I still kept going to Woodrow Wilson in East San Diego, travelling by bus. My mother said, "You keep on going out there boy because you're learning." I was only getting Bs and Cs in courses, but the content was more challenging. I was starring on the J.V. football team, and I was going to play for Hoover High School, an all white team. The school authorities found out I had moved away and told me I had to transfer back to inner-city San Diego.

So, in eighth grade, I went back to Memorial JHS. Urban junior high schools then, like today, were run like jails. It had a fence seven feet tall around it and lots of rules for the "inmates." We had two evaluations, one for citizenship and one for academics. I got As in both. In fact, I became vice-president of the school. But, I also had come back from the outside, so at first I had to defend my leadership position. The school was about half minority—blacks and Chicanos—and half working-class whites. There were a few gangs, and some bathrooms you couldn't safely go into. You could buy a joint—marijuana cigarette—for a nickel.

The school had a nutrition break because they thought all those poor kids needed to get some orange juice and snacks. That's where the fights took place, early in the morning. The bigger ones beat up on the smaller ones for protection dues. Of course, you had to fight back, even if you lost, or they would never leave you alone.

By eighth grade most young black males were doing some kind of work to help out their families. I got a job at the naval base as a

"Heavy-Laborer" on the "graveyard shift," 12 PM to 7 AM, cleaning submarine tanks. I would go to school, go to football or track practice, sleep a few hours and go to work. Homework had to be done in study halls. Later, I found less heavy work that fit in better with sports and studies.

The 1989 Carnegie Corporation report titled "Turning Points: Preparing American Youth for the 21st Century," called for a complete overhaul of American junior high and middle schools. Of the seventeen million adolescents in sixth through ninth grade, nearly seven million are considered "at risk" for trouble with the law, dropping out, drug or alchohol addiction, or teen parenthood. As my interviews with gang members in Chapters 4 and 5 demonstrate, such problems, including joining a gang, usually begin as early as age ten. If we are serious about helping American youth pass safely through the risky early adolescent years, we must be talking about a major role for public schools.

The mismatch between what young students need and want and what schools offer is greatest in the middle school years. As adolescents, they are exploring their emerging sexual identity while separating from family, preparing for adult roles of the future, and forging a moral values system. These changes are manifested in needs to try out new behaviors, form new group relationships, test adult authority, and dream expansive dreams. Traditional junior high schools spend much time and energy thwarting those very needs and manifestations.

Typically, we send twelve or thirteen year old students to huge, warehoused, centralized schools, where they suddenly face larger classes, many different courses and teachers, a huge new population of students, and long lists of behavior control rules. As William Glasser, M.D. described the mismatch: "It is this lack of access to power in the academic classes that is so frustrating to students because it comes just at the time when students are beginning to experience the increased need for power which is part of normal development" (Glasser 1986, 63).

That mismatch causes problems for adolescents from many backgrounds. For poor inner-city boys, it can be a recipe for disaster. In junior high and middle schools, tracking settles in, in earnest. Yet 49 percent of thirteen year old black boys start this next critical phase one or more years below their modal grade. Educational researcher Kawanza Kunjufu looked at the school records of twenty randomly selected young black males who had been in the same school for five years. He compared Iowa Reading Test scores from third grade and seventh grade. Some students who scored very high in the third grade "collapsed academically" by the end of seventh. Even academically gifted—or perhaps, especially academically gifted—young boys of color do not necessarily follow their early path of promise in school (Prothrow-Stith 1991, 165–6).

Outside of schools, the dangers of street life heat up for twelve and thirteen year olds. At this point, police begin to harass and assert authority over them; young black males are routinely stopped and searched. Storekeepers eye them suspiciously. Older citizens cross over to the other side of the street to avoid them. The realities of threats from gangs and from the police create natural responses of fear and bravado. Narcissism, also natural to early adolescence, further alienates teachers, parents and other adults.

Bonding into close-knit groups is typical, normal behavior, whether of suburban teenyboppers roaming the malls or of young initiates in gangs protecting their turf. Prejudices already learned at home or elsewhere will tend to be reinforced in those groups, unless there is a concerted effort by adults to counteract racism, sexism, intolerance for handicaps and bullying.

Successful junior high and middle schools value these early adolescent changes and needs through supporting positive group bonding and using structures such as cooperative learning teams to promote self-esteem and respect for others. We will return to the Carnegie recommendations, to team teaching and cooperative learning strategies, in Chapter 7.

For myself, our club "The Lucky 13" provided mutual support. We had to stand up together at least once, when "The Yellow Jackets" challenged us as a rival "gang." But we were not a gang. We got together and spun dreams of what we would do and what we could be. And we all basically reached those dreams to some extent. We had a few teachers who helped, family who supported us, and most essentially, each other. By contrast, Deborah Prothrow-Stith described the way urban youth sometimes join gangs and the drug trade, flash expensive clothes and cars, lavish gifts on their girlfriends and babies, as playing out the American Dream with a script written by adolescents.

HIGH SCHOOL: SEARCH FOR PURPOSE, ROLES AND WORK

If the mismatch in junior high is between early adolescent needs and the strictures of a repressive environment, then the mismatch in high school is between emerging adult roles and diminished real world opportunities. The young men and women who chose gangs usually saw no other viable alternatives. Failing or bored in school, they dropped out. Looking for work, they found nothing available for a black, male high school dropout.

I was extremely lucky that I had some other alternatives. Work was plentiful in post-war San Diego. Half the students in my junior high school were never going to high school, never mind college. It was a big thing, just going to high school. They had a good vocational education system for working students then. You turned sixteen, went over to the naval base or airplane factory and got a full-time job.

My high school was not great, but I saw ways to negotiate it successfully. I had broken out of the mold. I took college-prep courses—even German—despite what others thought I should aspire to. I was even dating a policeman's daughter—mixing with well-to-do blacks. When my girlfriend's mother would drive me home, I used to get out one block away from where I lived. I refused to be poor, and I refused to be on welfare. When I worked, as a junior high school student, we lost some support that my mother would have gotten. Most of the other black kids normally quit and never made it out of high school, but good jobs were available. Opportunities in sports—I played football and track—took us beyond the boundaries of our immediate communities. Many of those opportunities have dried up in inner-city neighborhoods today.

I had two teachers who took an interest in me and helped me. An ex-naval officer who was also my math teacher would ask me if he could be my surrogate dad for various father-son sports events. That meant a lot. My auto shop teacher had high academic standards for us. Before we could begin actual hands on work on the cars, we had to be able to write down our plans on paper, strengthening math reasoning and writing skills.

I wrote for the school newspaper and dreamed of being some sort of writer. My friend from the Lucky 13, David, said, "Let me

take your story to Miss _____," the head of the English Department. She called me in and said, "Son, you know, you're a hard
working boy. You go on to Convair [the airplane factory] and get
you a good job. You could become lead man." I said, "Yes, Ma'am,"
thinking to myself, "To hell with you, I'm going to college!" That's
what I mean when I say, you never asked for help from white
teachers in school.

That story may sound like the Dark Ages, but in 1992, when
open enrollment came to Massachusetts schools, there was outrage
in the city of Springfield over a letter written to the neighboring
Longmeadow School Committee by a Springfield high school
teacher who lived in that community. In this letter, dated March 4,
1992, this teacher was warning her hometown against the dangers
of enrolling Springfield teenagers:

> As an English teacher at Central High School, Springfield, I am acutely
> aware of the differences in the curriculum in the two school systems,
> resulting in an extremely wide gap. My Central tenth graders have never
> been taught the basics of grammar, as is the case with the curriculum of
> Longmeadow. . . . This . . . will slow down the excellent pace our Long-
> meadow students have always enjoyed, thus diluting their education.
>
> A second valid argument against the School Choice plan is the differ-
> ences in socioeconomic life styles. Most of these children's families do not
> own a home or car. When they see Longmeadow (They do not at present
> know where it is) they will jump to the conclusion that we are all rich. How
> will they respond to this? . . .
>
> But perhaps more important than the reduced educational level, or the
> fights in our schools is the stark reality that Springfield students are
> extremely promiscuous. This, in and of itself may not be that alarming,
> but what is of supreme urgency is the fact that they are transmitting
> syphilis, gonorrhea, and most frightening, HIV. . . . Is this what you want
> to bring into the Longmeadow public schools? Is the School Board ready
> for the contagion these students, their diseases and their fighting will
> produce?

This letter was made public in the local newspaper and on local
television. Under pressure from citizens, students, other teachers
and administrators, that teacher eventually resigned.

Adolescence is a long stretch of "hard time," from about age
twelve to eighteen, during which a child develops into an adult.
Trying on adult roles and searching for meaningful work are a

crucial part of that passage, as well as the other quests mentioned before. The American world of work has never made much room for African American males, except during the industrial boom of the World War II era. Since 1955, twice as many blacks have been unemployed as whites, a ratio that persists today. Without hope of decent work, it is very hard for a young man to find motivation to stay in school; and shrinking opportunities in factory jobs make schooling more essential now than ever before for economic survival. High schools must face these realities and encourage urban youth to stay in school through meaningful work apprenticeships, fulfilling roles serving others, challenging, reality-based curricula providing useful skills, and athletic teams and other extracurricular activities that build pride. Above all, high schools must abolish tracking, hold the highest expectations for poor and minority students, and actively combat the "contagion" of racism.

TEACHER PREPARATION AND EDUCATIONAL RESEARCH

We have already explored some of the shortcomings of educational research in the sections on "Education and Equality" and "Race and Class." For these shortcomings, schools of education must be held accountable. Since I am myself a professor at a school of education, I describe these problems both from the inside and from the outside. As an African American male going to school, I saw the face of racism at its most cruel, when it took the form of a teacher narrowing the options or smothering the hope of a child. As an education professor, I counsel undergraduate future teachers who have experienced almost nothing of the world of urban classrooms that they will enter, and who are ill-prepared to teach effectively or hold high expectations for children so different from themselves.

Even with the best intentions, student teachers may harbor unconscious prejudices that they are not aware of. In an Illinois study, sixty-six student teachers were told to teach math concepts to groups of four pupils—two white and two black. All of the pupils were of equal, average intelligence, but the student teachers were told that in their group of four, a particular white and a particular black child were intellectually gifted. The student teachers were monitored through one-way glass to see how they reinforced their students' efforts. The "superior" white children received, on average, two positive reinforcements for every one negative. The "average" white children received one positive for every one negative. The "average" black children received one positive reinforcement for every 1.5 negative. And the "superior" black children received, on average, one positive reinforcement for every 3.5 negative ones! Why would this happen in this country today? Academic excellence in black students was being discouraged. These were young, idealistic future teachers "probably blind to their own cultural biases" (Prothrow-Stith 1991, 165).

In an example of educational research that has profound implications for positive changes for teachers and schools, Harvard Professor Ronald Ferguson conducted a five-year study of the Texas public school system, including more than 2.4 million students and 150,000 teachers in nearly 900 school districts. His conclusions supported the common-sense assumption that "better teachers produce better students and better teachers require higher salaries, [therefore] spending more money on teachers produces better students." This study revealed "the link between teacher quality and student test scores, and the link between better teachers and districts which pay more and have better resources." The other best predictor of student performance (as Coleman discovered in 1966) was the education level of the parents. "It's basically whether your parents can read and whether your teacher can read," said Ferguson (reported in *The Boston Globe*, May 12, 1991, 38–39).

The education and training of teachers is critical, and it is to those future teachers, especially, that we address this book. For many different reasons, including inadequate preparation for the challenges of the job, more than half of those who enter teaching drop out within five years. We have to do better than that in this country.

Certainly, higher hopes for urban youth also rest on more minority teachers in their classrooms and, therefore, on more minority college graduates. Disturbingly, the recent trend is in the opposite direction. Hard economic times, diminished federal loans, doubling and tripling of public college tuition, and increased racism on predominantly white campuses are all to blame. Almost half of college-bound black students come from families with incomes below $12,000 versus only 10 percent of white students (Gibbs 1988, xiv). Andrew Billingsley suggests that members of the black middle class, because most are first generation, have a precarious toehold on security. Even in the best of times, it is hard to take the risk that going into debt for a college education will pay off (Billingsley 1992).

More blacks are graduating from high school and scoring better on college entrance exams today, but fewer are going to college. Low-income black high school graduates attending college peaked in 1976 at 40 percent, but dropped to 30 percent by 1988. Of the black middle class, 53 percent attended college in 1976 versus only 36 percent in 1988 (*Newsweek*, January 29, 1990, 75).

At the University of Massachusetts at Amherst during the past five years, "Black non-Hispanic" enrollment declined by 23 percent—more than twice the rate at which nonminority enrollment declined. The percentage of doctorates awarded to minorities nationally has also declined in the past decade. Doctorates awarded to blacks dropped from 4.6 percent of the total in 1980 to 3.6 percent in 1989, largely due to a 35 percent decline in the number of black men earning doctorates (Gentry et al. 1991, 23). On March 11, 1993, ABC News reported that the proportion of minority Ph.D.'s had dwindled to 2 percent for blacks and 3 percent for Latinos.

The largest share of doctorates earned by minorities (except Asians) are awarded in the field of education. In 1989, 27 percent of all doctorates awarded to Hispanics and 48 percent of those awarded to blacks were in education. But at UMass Amherst, for example, graduate programs targeted for termination during the fiscal crisis of 1990–91 were preponderantly in education, as well as health and other human services that have also trained a large proportion of minority professionals. Two programs within the School of Education that served more than 70 percent of black graduate students at the university were eliminated.

Thus, in addition to the other mismatches we identified facing minority children in urban schools, we add the declining numbers of minority teachers. This dilemma was addressed recently in an academic area where the effects of institutional racism and sexism are most evident: science and mathematics. Reported Lynn Arthur Steen in "Mathematics for All Americans:"

In twenty-three of the nation's twenty-five largest public school systems .
. . total enrollment of minorities is over 50 percent. By the year 2000, 40
percent of children in public schools will be black or Hispanic. . . . Yet, three
quarters of U.S. citizens who receive Ph.D. degrees in mathematics are
white males. According to a recent projection of the U.S. work force in the
year 2000, only 15 percent of the young people entering the labor force will
be white males. (NCTM 1990 Yearbook, *Teaching and Learning Mathematics
in the 1990s*, 130)

On the positive side of that equation, although the Rand Corporation found that minorities experience "consistent patterns of
unequal opportunities to learn math and science," the College
Board found a strong correlation between studying mathematics
and college attendance among minority students: "Minorities who
take high school geometry enroll in college at almost the same rate
as whites" (*Report on Education Research*, October 3, 1990, 5).

When I was approaching high school graduation, I saw that the
only route to a college degree for me was the G.I. Bill. I read all the
books on colleges and how to apply. I learned that if you put your
name on the top of the list at your draft board, you got drafted for
two years (if you volunteered, it was for three years). My mother
had by now moved to Pasadena. So, my goal was to go to an
affordable junior college—Pasadena Junior College. I enlisted (was
drafted) and served in Korea, after the fighting stopped. During
my training, I had a chance for the first time to read, to visit the
library and read every book I was interested in. When I returned,
I began my college education.

Can I interject a small caveat and digression here? When I was
at a fancy wedding on Nantucket a few years ago, a sweet, old-
wealth white lady said to me, "Black people need to make some
money. Why don't you be like Bill Cosby?" Now, I appreciate her
wish that my people could do better, but to think that the solution
to the problems of poor and minority Americans is to all be like Bill
Cosby—or Michael Jordan—is rather unrealistic. Similarly, to say
that the solution to the barriers faced by young black males is to
follow *my* path is also unrealistic. I was very stubborn and very
lucky. I never gave up hope. I include my story and others like it
to humanize the struggles we see faced by young black men in
inner cities. Not everyone can find his way out. But if *everyone* loses

hope, everyone's world—white and black together—will deteriorate.

When I returned to Pasadena, California, after the army, I started college and worked part-time. I needed to find a "school boy's" job at the Post Office. First, I had to take whatever I could get, such as painting mailboxes. But I persisted, and later got assigned what we would call a "school boy's" job—part-time and not physically demanding, so you could still do your studies.

After completing two years at Pasadena City College, I took a job with the Army Corps of Engineers. Then, I went on to Cal State Los Angeles, majoring in education. Eventually, I took a year off from the Army Corps of Engineers to finish my degree and was working part-time as an assistant teacher in Pasadena Junior High School. I taught Algebra and also helped students in the special needs (kick-out) room. There, I saw how it was for most kids. The white students were doing fine. The Asian students went to the temple after school and did their homework for the next day or the next week! The black kids didn't know what to do, and nobody helped them.

In Algebra, I had this little, black "hard-headed" boy who was always getting into something, hitting people and fooling around. I used to try to "con" him into learning something. While they were taking an Algebra quiz I'd go around and say, "Why don't you try this?" The kids would say, "You're *helping* me?" I would reply, "We're here to learn. This quiz grade isn't as important." So, the class began to come around some, and I had this little boy learning something.

On one test paper, he got an A. I asked him, "Will you tell me how you got this answer?" He said, "First, would you write the A in ink?" He had been messed over so many times, he didn't trust anybody. He showed me how he solved the problem, and I had him show his solution to some other students. Eventually, I got everyone helping somebody else—even the Asian-American students who were more aloof. I would say to them, "Would you do me a favor and show so-and-so? Because people learn things differently."

That story from my first teaching job has all the elements of "The Hope Factor." The students who are most hungry for learning feel most defiant when they are shut out. Once you gain their trust and they begin to learn, you can have them helping others. Added to the self-esteem of successful learning is the self-esteem gained in helping others. Ultimately, it is more than just self-esteem. It is having a purpose in life and a reason for living. That need and goal is bigger than black and white, rich and poor. That is the connection with helping others.

chapter three

Westside Stories

❏ ❏ ❏

"TIME IS RUNNING OUT"

During the 1960s, tremendous social tides of change in this country, crested in the Civil Rights Movement and the War on Poverty. Black Americans everywhere were looking for change with new hope. The times were changing for me as well. Settled in Pasadena, California, I got married, bought a house and had a son, finished my undergraduate degree and founded Westside Study Center.

In the four years that I was director, Westside evolved from a neighborhood tutoring center to a wide-reaching community action agency working with Pasadena schools, businesses, police and courts, churches, universities, and social agencies. What began by serving the education needs of local black youth evolved to include people from every imaginable background, all races and all levels of education: black, white, Hispanic and Asian Americans; school dropouts and university professors; shopkeepers and chairs of boards; cops on the beat and attorneys.

At Westside, we gained the trust of gang members and got them reconnected to meaningful work and education. Symbolically and in fact, we got them to give up their war jackets for the college blazers of Westside. On the pocket of our maroon jackets, which were earned through service and achievement, was an hour glass with our motto, "Time Is Running Out." The Watts Riots of August, 1965, which erupted just over a year after Westside began, gave immediate urgency to our motto.

At Westside, we had older youth tutoring younger ones, and adults teaching each other. We trained young men and sent them out to companies, seeking jobs for others, when they themselves had never gone beyond the few square blocks of their neighborhood. We held community open forums where hundreds of residents came out to hear peaceful debates between groups as disparate as the Black Nationalists and the John Birch Society. We travelled to Washington, D.C., to make a sensitivity training film, "Black Anger" for Bell and Howell. Our community liaisons worked to stop local crimes, to prevent gang violence, and were on the street keeping people calm when Watts erupted.

In 1964, I took a leave of absence from the Army Corps of Engineers to finish my undergraduate degree in education at Cal State Los Angeles. That spring, with several other friends, I started a community tutoring program, Westside Study Center, located in the VFW hall. I also taught part-time in Pasadena Junior High School. From my experiences in education and work, I formed my own basic philosophy that also became the philosophy of Westside: "The Hope Factor."

The first tenet of "The Hope Factor" is that everyone can learn. The key is confidence and motivation found through trust—trust that you can show your weaknesses and learn from and go beyond them. Second, everyone can benefit from helping someone else. Self-esteem emerges through doing something useful for someone else. Third, everyone wants to be a part of something. Young people join gangs to belong, to be loved, and to be needed. When you establish trust with them and show them better alternatives, they don't need gangs anymore.

So, for example, while I was teaching at Pasadena Junior High, I was finding more and more students coming to me at the "kickout room" to get help and tutor each other. Problems the administration had with fires set in the bathrooms and the selling of dope nearby were solved once I could reach the students and develop trust. Similarly, at our tutoring headquarters at Westside Study Center, the positive word spread. By the end of the second year, we had over 200 youth of various ages coming to the center day and night. I never did go back to the Army Corps of Engineers.

IMPLEMENTING THE HOPE FACTOR

In 1965 Pasadena, California, had grown from a sleepy retirement community in the western end of the San Gabriel Valley of Los Angeles County to an important city of 180,000 people, 15 percent of whom were black. Home of such famous institutions as Jet Propulsion Laboratory, California Institute of Technology and the Rose Bowl parade, Pasadena had more than smog and freeway construction to denote its urban status. In 1969, Pasadena became the first school district west of the Mississippi to be sued by the Justice Department for segregated schools.

When we founded Westside Study Center, we were motivated by the desire to do something about the serious problems in our community, especially education. Westside Study Center became many things to many people: a place on North Fair Oaks Avenue where local residents made more than a thousand visits a week; a group of people, black and white, working together to make positive changes; a coordinated series of programs emphasizing education and job development reaching hard-core poverty persons; and a vehicle through which people could help others and help themselves.

We did not have to search out people in need. In the census tracts around the Center, one out of every three families earned less than a poverty level income. One out of four adults was looking for a job. Washington Elementary School, just a block away, enrolled less than ten percent whites, reflecting a serious separation of races in the school system. That system failed with the many blacks who dropped out before completing high school; and a majority of blacks who graduated could not read beyond the fifth grade level ("Neighborhood Social Diagnostic Survey," Community Redevelopment Agency of Pasadena, April 1967).

In three long years, Westside became a viable organization because it grew and built upon its established strengths. From the first, the staff had an unusual dedication to their primary task of helping people. Incorporating that dedication into its own organization, the staff operated on a career lattice model: hard core unemployed youths who showed promise were brought in as aides; as soon as possible, aides were promoted to assistants and as high as component coordinators. Many of the Westside staff, including myself, were enrolled in courses at Pasadena City College or Cal State Los Angeles in order to improve our own skills and to gain the academic degrees that would expand employment opportunities.

A second source of strength depended upon a coordinated approach so that Westside's educational and communications services both supported and gained support from its job development and counseling services. For example, when a youth telephoned from the courtroom after an arrest, Westside staff would speak on his behalf. Usually municipal and juvenile judges would assign the youth to the Center rather than to jail (an idea whose time has come *again* under Attorney General Janet Reno). Then the staff would talk over the youth's problems, perhaps arranging for special tutoring and for his return to school. Often a lack of money had caused the initial problem, and Westside located part-time work. By providing a sense of support and hope in many areas of need, Westside could affect someone's life direction.

A third key to Westside's success was its broad range of active supporters—unmatched by any other agency working in the city. Westside staff worked with men who had more items on their arrest records than entries on their resumes; and the same staff met with businessmen and city officials in racial-sensitivity sessions. Tutoring drew adults seeking basic literacy, elementary school children having difficulties assimilating the white culture of their reading texts, high school dropouts attending special classes in order to earn a general education diploma, workers seeking vocational skills, and college-level students seeking special training in writing. Businessmen, school board members, and retired citizens stopped by to see what was happening. Often, they stayed to volunteer their services.

Whether the Study Center had outside financial support or relied upon the staff to volunteer their time, Westside had convinced poor people in the Los Angeles County area that it offered more than a meaningless promise and another referral. The staff "took care of business." Similarly, businessmen learned to respect the work of the Center and trust its continued interest in the persons placed in jobs. Westside "guaranteed" the people it trained and placed. Our staff would come in and work with a company on any problem that arose with the new employee. Organizations such as the courts, the city police, and city schools asked Westside for assistance in dealing with poor people.

Strongly motivated to make our organization survive and grow, committed to our dream of creating a vehicle for growth and change, the staff at Westside built learning into our whole operation. Never content to repeat past successes, we continually faced situations and problems requiring new skills, new contacts, and new risks. Experienced staff trained new aides. The efficiency of the organization was never defined simply in terms of numbers of lessons tutored, jobs found, or counseling sessions conducted. Those tasks had meaning only if they helped people to survive and find hope in the system. That purpose gave a unity of meaning to the Center as it sought ongoing support and a chance to affect change in Pasadena.

BRIEF HISTORY

For the first year, Westside Study Center operated as a volunteer tutoring and counseling service. We began simply with the idea of helping children to read. Volunteers from the community and from local high schools and colleges were recruited to tutor children and youth on a one-to-one basis. Initially the Study Center focused on reading, arithmetic and writing. Too many black children had been turned off by the standard white-oriented curriculum of Pasadena's schools and the too-often indifference of the teachers.

As more people came to us who needed help or who had skills to volunteer, Westside accepted a larger task. Finding part-time employment might keep a youth in high school, where his problems had less to do with learning than with his own self-concept. Sometimes the key lay in a discussion with the school's counselor who was not communicating well with a child. Often Westside staff talked with parents in an effort to enlist their help in supporting a child's study. Sometimes the staff had to work with a tutor who, for example, knew calculus but could not relate to black children. Soon a large proportion of time by the staff went toward arranging, mediating and counseling between other volunteer tutors or agency officials and tutees. It was clear that Westside would need some full-time, paid staff.

During the summer of 1966, the Center received summer "crash" funds from the Office of Economic Opportunity (OEO). With a grant of $50,000, the Center proved that its pioneering work in education, job development, counseling, community services and communication could be expanded into significant and inter-related programs. More than seventy jobs, for example, were found for adults in the Pasadena area during the summer.

I knew from the start, however, that summer crash poverty program funds were a mixed blessing for the Center. If you raise people's hopes with a summer job, what do you say to them in the fall when the money fades away? Westside had to stay alive on hope and private donations and volunteers. Our low-cost tutoring program continued into the next fall with over forty tutors and eighty students. Most of the staff who had worked during that summer stayed on without funds. The spring of 1967 was a building period; new projects and new programs were developed on a shoestring. Local business pledges and private support grew steadily.

Again in the summer of 1967, crash funds became available from OEO. But $10,000 provided only enough to operate a job develop-ment component. We employed youths as aides in teams to contact local firms and ferret out job opportunities. The Westside staff counseled both prospective employees and employers in pre- and post-job training. With their experience from the previous summer, Westside aides established good working relationships with many Pasadena firms so that counseling could reach people before on-the-job problems had accumulated. As a result, Westside placed more than one hundred persons in meaningful and continuing jobs.

Because of that success and because of growing support within the Northwest community, Pasadena's Commission on Human Need and Opportunity supported continuing the program for three more months. During that time, sixty-seven placements were made. In the meantime, private donations and volunteer time supported the other components of a rounded community action agency.

As of the summer of 1968, the Westside Study Center operated from three sites and six small buildings in the poverty area. Its work fell into four main functions: (1) job development, (2) education, (3) community services, and (4) public relations. Each component had a coordinator with several aides and Neighborhood Youth Corps clerk-typists under his guidance, as well as several volunteers who did work ranging from typing addresses to providing comprehensive management consultation. Westside's budget ran about $15,000 per month, including $2,000 per month from pledged private donations. Those figures, however, grossly understated its impact, which was augmented by the many unpaid volunteers who helped Westside not only at the Center but also in the city.

Only the job development component had federal support, and it had achieved an astonishing record of success because it had worked with the other supporting services. Tutoring at all levels remained the most common meeting ground where blacks and other poor residents learned about the Center as a place to seek help. In the tutoring program, people from outside and inside the immediate community came together to make a meaningful contribution of their time and skills. A Caltech aeronautical engineer volunteered to teach math for us and donated his consulting fees from one day a month. He made learning math fun and exciting for everyone. Other Caltech faculty and students came to see what was happening at Westside and joined in.

High school students from an elite private school in San Marino joined the tutoring program. In 1968, on the day of Martin Luther King Jr.'s assassination, they came to the Center and manned the telephones while our staff went out to keep people calm and talk to the neighborhood. During the summers, young people from Philadelphia came to work at Westside through the American Friends Service Committee. The Quakers' greatest contribution to us was teaching young people how to talk things out. In a typical ghetto family, parents couldn't spend much time conversing with children. We learned a lot from the Quaker meeting style of listening to each other and finding consensus.

Our community services component developed a close and effective relationship with the Pasadena Police Department and with municipal and juvenile courts. During 1968, Center staff members counseled more than 164 individuals. In most cases, those persons were released by the courts under the recognizance of the Center. That service won respect and support from a part of the community not reached in a helpful way by any other agency. Whatever we needed to know about juvenile law, we learned. Some of our formerly "baddest" street guys took pride in their abilities to help out youngsters in the courts and to make recommendations to the judge.

The public relations component coordinated the growing activities—speeches, basic encounter sessions, open forums, and news releases—through which Westside communicated with the wider community. We held Open Forum debates and discussions on an outdoor stage—a loading dock at a warehouse donated to the Center. I wanted our youth to learn to think for themselves. Our basic rule was, "Everyone has a right to express their opinion." No matter what their philosophy, we listened to the speakers we had invited. I urged our young people to research the issues. They went to the library and read articles on the topics. I wasn't interested in promoting the kind of militant conformity of some black nationalist groups. But they were welcome to participate and state their views.

When a need appeared, we tried to meet it. "Late Start" provided adult education, and some of our school dropouts reconnected with education themselves by teaching adults basic skills. We ran workshops for women re-entering the job market. We organized a women's discussion group centered around the problems their men had with education and employment. Sometimes, if a street youth got a job and settled down, his wife or girlfriend might have trouble adjusting to his new, more boring lifestyle. Before, part of her self-image depended on his "homeboy" street reputation, and a "homebody" was less attractive. In order to support his new work or education efforts, she needed to rethink her ideas of status and seek other goals in their relationship.

It is important to repeat that the Westside Study Center staff were not trained professionals, but volunteers, aides, leaders in training who were taking part in their own career lattice of education and job improvement. I was the closest we had to a professional, and I was learning on the job as much as anyone.

When a street youth or gang member came to the Center, first we would talk to him and find out his needs and potential contributions. Usually, he would begin as a tutor to a younger person and thus develop his own confidence and self-esteem. His educational and job training problems were addressed in a coordinated way. We used the "mirror technique" to get trainees to see themselves in the eyes of their prospective employers: "Look at yourself. Would you hire you?" Every week there would be job counseling sessions. I would say to the job trainees, "See if you can go out there and con the Man out of a job." If you could counsel and support that person to stay with that job for six months, he was "over." In many cases, a black man would get himself fired or quit *before* the Man would fire him in order to preserve his dignity. But if he could stay with the job for six months, he would have bought into the system and acquired hope that he could succeed.

At Westside, neighborhood youth would work part-time in the various program components. They might tutor children or illiterate adults; they might help search out jobs within the community; they might go to the courts to counsel young offenders. Regularly, I had promising trainees—our "Junior Executives"—serve as coordinators-for-the-day of the various components. They would put on a jacket and tie, sit at a desk, act professional and do a fantastic job. Those who had proved themselves through service and personal growth became members of our Westside "gang," and won the right to wear our maroon blazer. Through self-help and helping others, we constructed the hope factor for all our lives and for the surrounding community.

SELF-HELP AND THE HOPE FACTOR

Self-help—pulling yourself up by your own bootstraps—was a complex notion since it had to come from within before it could be sold as an idea to others. It involved the subtle problem of creating the power to control at least a part of one's own life and a part of one's own community—a power which lay at the heart of individual freedom. And it involved a cruel paradox. From the point of view of many in the ghetto, anyone who had boots with straps had already escaped. How could he relate to those who needed help?

At Westside, our answer depended upon our staff operating one step ahead of those who came for assistance. Recognizing the importance of trust as a prerequisite for effective communication, Center staff talked about their recent struggles to learn. Tutors who gained the confidence of a child in trouble at school created an atmosphere of hope and positive direction that proved effective despite a lack of resources and professional training. On the other side, tutors often learned a great deal. As they talked to the tutees, they discovered that difficulty with learning often sprang from insensitive teaching.

The idea of self-help was as simple and as complex as anything about the Center. The staff had to inspire hope and motivation—an illusion of power. Then, students who thought they could not learn and tutors who thought they could not teach would have a chance to discover their power to help themselves and others. For black males to admit they could not read meant admitting stupidity and failure. Self-help allowed tutors and staff to tell of their own hang-ups, fears and failures and build trust. They saw themselves as being in the process of overcoming those difficulties. By emphasizing change, Westside helped create an atmosphere of hope that won an indispensable motivation.

Self-help depended upon a staff that ranged from youth aides holding their first jobs to component coordinators who had considerable experience but lacked college diplomas for a professional position. The staff—including myself, the associate director and most aides—were either in college or planning to return. The Center used ideas of New Careers and paraprofessionals before the terms were popularized (Pearl and Riessman 1965). Unless the staff was helping itself to learn and helping itself by advancing from aide to assistant and from coordinator to well-paying jobs in industry, that staff could scarcely sell the concept of self-help to others.

The resulting turnover of staff and confusion in the management chart was more than compensated for by the rapport with those who came to Westside because they trusted us. The contrast with established welfare and service agencies went beyond an atmosphere of openness. Most agencies assumed that their clients lacked power. The first solution to a problem would be to call for a new survey. The implication was that poor people could not even grasp their own plight. Thus, any alleviation must come from the established power blocs, who would—presumably—mend their ways when told about the extent of deprivation and discrimination.

As a result, most official agencies fostered and supported one of the most damaging aspects of ghetto pathology, "learned helplessness." Repeated frustrations created a helplessness and anger that turned many black youth against even trying to make it. Why struggle in a system that prevented success and that could not be destroyed? Before people could put their energies and thoughts into learning to read or holding a meaningful job, they had to see some chance to win, some avenue through which they could get ahead. Without a vision of possible control over their own future, self-help was meaningless. Yet most agencies, most police officers, most welfare workers, most church groups, most city officials, most school teachers in Pasadena implied in their tone and actions that blacks could not control their own lives without assistance from a white world that was paternalistic at best and often hostile.

Self-help, when supported with enough tutoring, enough counseling, and enough encouragement so that individuals could see some positive accomplishments, worked to change both actions and attitudes. In personal terms, the changes were often dramatic. A street youth who had expressed bitterness and anger at conditions became interested and concerned while tutoring a third grader with reading or spelling. At Westside Study Center, we operated on the assumption that hope is contagious.

WESTSIDE STORIES

The young men who came to Westside Study Center were usually members of one of four different local gangs. Often they had special skills, but not skills that had been recognized in school or gotten them jobs. We had a few fundamental rules at the Center: no weapons, no drugs, no parties among different gangs. In this chapter I want to share the stories of two former gang members, "Junior Boy" and "Duke."

In Spring of 1968, I was in Washington, D.C. with my Job Development Coordinator on a fund-raising trip. This was just two weeks after the assassination of Martin Luther King, Jr. We were contacted by the Human Development Institute in Atlanta, a subsidiary of Bell and Howell, to make a movie, "Black Anger," for their sensitivity training programs for industry. Could we come to Atlanta the next day with five of our coordinators?

As I described previously, you earned your Westside jacket. Similarly, you "earned your travelling time," the chance to put on the jacket and travel representing Westside. After our coordinators paid their dues and earned their jackets, they gained a wider vision of what their lives could be. They began to think "like a college student." Again, once they paid their dues, did something outstanding on their own, and earned their jacket, they became a part of the system wider than Westside.

John, "Junior Boy," hadn't earned his Westside jacket yet, but we needed another coordinator in order to make the film for HDI. I called the Center and told them to "suit up Junior Boy." The staff bought him a jacket, black shoes, tie and attaché case out of their own pockets. They got him a ticket—John had never been on a plane before. When the plane took off, he practically pulled that seat out of the floor. But he made the trip, and he became my eyes and ears while we were in Atlanta. I said, "We are a team. We're here to work, not to party." John kept track of everybody and everything for me. He could look around a room and size up the whole situation. He "read" people very well.

John was seventeen years old, a mountain of a kid. He said very little to people but had a photographic memory and took in everything that was happening. He was quietly very smart. After our experience in Atlanta, John was never the same. He was no longer programmed for jail; he had different needs. He had gotten a taste of another world, a world larger than the few square blocks he had ruled in Pasadena. He wanted a share of success in the larger world he had glimpsed. Soon after the Atlanta trip, he became Assistant Coordinator for Job Development at Westside. He got his GED and went on to Pasadena City College. Years later, I saw John and his wife in San Diego. He came up and hugged me. He had gotten a job as a supervisor at the Rose Bowl. He made it.

Not all our stories at Westside had happy endings. One of Junior Boy's friends on the staff, "Duke," ended up back in jail. Duke was the subject of an unpublished case study: Born in 1948, he never experienced a stable family life. His mother, unmarried, had arrived from Arkansas, shortly before his birth. His natural father from Pasadena provided some support, but spent little time with him. The three most influential members of his family were his mother, his maternal grandmother, and his maternal great grandmother, with whom he lived. All worked as domestics, and they had never been on welfare. "Cousins" in the neighborhood looked after Duke when he was younger.

Although he stayed in school for twelve years, Duke could barely read a newspaper. He had no skills readily sellable on the job market, and his physical strengths had little value in the machine era. At the age of thirteen he had his first formal confrontation with the police. His arrest record included marijuana possession, destruction of property, suspicion of robbery, and an alleged assault on a police officer; and he had been tried for attempted murder. Duke recognized his problems with his temper, and that he quickly leaped to the support of his friends. He felt a gun was a necessary protection.

Duke spent his time hustling—he never held a middle-class job. For a time, he was paid by the police to act as a control on the behavior of his friends. He was viewed by the police as a "ring leader" and by his Juvenile Probation Officer as a "unique guy" and "natural leader."

Duke came to Westside with the help of a "cousin," a respected businessman in the black community. He became a community relations assistant at the Center in November, 1967. The job, which paid $1.50 an hour, four hours a day, was the first time he had worked where he was expected to be some place on time to do certain specified things. The job involved him with the police and the courts in a new way. Parents of young people arrested in the area would call the Study Center, and then Duke, among others, would go to jail and to the police to talk to and about the prisoner and his alleged offense.

In the case of juveniles, he would go to court with the youth and tell the judge the results of the investigation he had made regarding the boy's friends, his contacts in the community, and the possibility of his staying out of trouble in the future. Often, the juvenile courts would release the youth into Westside's custody.

Duke took pride in actually changing the judge's mind about the disposition of a youth. Duke and others like him learned to talk like a lawyer. In the case of young adults, Duke would make a similar report to the lawyer who was going to take the case. In addition, Duke made a financial investigation of the client and recommended to the attorney how much should be charged, based on ability to pay. Duke was proud that the lawyer would believe him and base the fees on his recommendation.

In spite of his competence and usefulness at Westside, Duke's troubles with the police did not end. His reputation, friends, and previous behavior pursued him. In 1968, Duke was arrested, convicted and given a sentence of five years to life.

At Westside, we had a staff that could reach people like Junior Boy and Duke whose lives were balanced precariously between success and defeat. They could empathize because they too had been abandoned by public institutions and white society. In Westside they mobilized their talents and frustrations—tutoring children, raising money, speaking in court, finding jobs, making a film, running encounter sessions. Young, gifted and black, their successes demonstrated the waste and neglect perpetrated by a racist society.

I remember a younger boy who came to the Center, brought by his mother. He was a kind of genius who always had negative experiences in school and wouldn't communicate with people in general. He was a nice looking boy with beautiful sisters. His father was living away in another house with several women. The situation was explosive for that boy. I was afraid he was going to shoot his father; he was smart enough to get in a lot of trouble. I went to juvenile court, to his probation officer, and when they asked my advice, I said, "Don't send him back to his mama. Get him out of this environment or you'll get that boy killed and the husband too." So they sent him to the youth "advance" camp to fight fires and do forestry conservation work.

In those days California Juvenile Authorities were pretty good about that. They didn't put him in with the hard-core group who were locked up all the time. For the first time in his life he had a pair of Levis and tennis shoes. I went and asked him, "Do you want to go home or to the advance camp?" He said to me, "I think I'd rather go to the camp, but don't tell my mother I said that to you." It is very sad that California stopped letting juvenile offenders fight fires because there was one death parachuting into a fire zone. If you were a ghetto parent, which way would you rather lose a son: shot on the streets in a drive-by, or fighting fires in camp?

I remember two people who came to Westside for help who never would have found each other through conventional agencies. A minister came to me and said that one of his parishioners, a wealthy middle-aged white lady, was badly in need of a purpose in life. Her husband didn't pay any attention to her, and she felt she had nothing to do. Her children were grown, and she was depressed.

We always had lists of people who needed some kind of help. A black man in our community had come in saying he needed someone to teach his mildly retarded wife basic survival skills such as shopping, taking the bus, having a bank account and paying bills. He was dying of cancer and realized he had always done things for her. Now, she needed to learn how to do more things for herself. She was quite capable. She had two beautiful children and kept her house neat as a pin.

So, the rich, unloved wife and the mildly-retarded wife got together to help each other. They met at the Center for lessons and went on field trips shopping or to the bank. The rich wife at first was frightened and felt she didn't know how to teach anybody anything. She would meet with me once a week, and I would suggest she try a certain approach, and when that didn't work, try something else. She had to learn "how to be a person"; she needed to understand someone else's needs and develop some feelings. After that, she became a part of the Center and the two women became great friends. The wealthier woman even brought her husband to see the Center. We didn't have to hustle people for donations. They would just come and see what we were doing and want to become a part of it.

In order to be effective, we had to keep in touch with what was happening out on the streets. Again, I did not want to foster a kind of group psychology where you were supposed to be an obedient soldier. But we had a "Red Alert" for serious situations that called for everyone's help. One day this little old Chinese lady from the neighborhood laundry called me up and said, "Mr. Gentry, they robbed me." We did not tolerate robberies in our own community. Although we used it very seldom, we called a "Red Alert," and everyone came to the Center to help. I said to the staff, "Find out who did it, now." In less than two hours, we found him. The Westside boys could find out in a minute what was going down by "jacking up" the pimps, who were always on the street and saw everything.

They brought the thief to Westside. He wasn't a part of Westside. I saw this frightened, short dude and I said to him, "We don't have robberies in this community. You can go to jail right now, or you can work for this lady in her laundry for two months." That was his "ultatomato." You know, he worked for her for free for two months and then kept on working for her for pay. Later, he and the little Chinese lady went into business together and opened a dry cleaners! They made some money, ran two businesses. He would come to Westside and tutor.

One of the stories about the street which had a sad ending did demonstrate how we could have positive relationships with the police. I had a hard and fast rule, gangs don't party together. One weekend, there was a party at a house where someone from L.A. lived downstairs. Nobody knew him very well, but they invited him to the party anyway. (We tried to convince young men to leave their guns at home when they went to parties.) They tried to do it right. This stranger got into a fight downstairs, and one of our young men, a nice kid who was planning to go to the police academy, was trying to break up the fight. The stranger pulled a gun and shot him point blank.

His friends didn't know that he was dead. They called the police and ambulance. They were losing their cool and got mad at the ambulance because they thought it took too long to get there. Some were shaking the ambulance. They went to the hospital. In the halls, when they found out the kid was dead, they grieved and were angry; someone insulted a nurse. There was tension and anger throughout the hospital. They wanted their young friend to be alive. The Pasadena police came and defused the situation. They were young cops who knew the victim. They took off their guns and laid them on the hood of the patrol car. They said, "If you want to fight, fight with your hands." Even the police were crying. They stopped the riot. County riot police were on their way, but they weren't needed. The next day, I went to the hospital and talked to the nurses. They knew Westside and understood the situation. Months later, on the day that Martin Luther King, Jr. was shot, people got together and expressed their grief and talked. There were no riots in Pasadena.

WESTSIDE'S CURRICULUM FOR THE COMMUNITY

The story of Westside Study Center revealed the failures of urban education in America. The Center showed most clearly what had not been done. Organized in response to a need for a broad range of self-help programs, it became a crucial learning center for relating the immediate needs of black children to the larger contexts of Pasadena and the national commitment to real equality for all citizens.

By the 1960s, Pasadena exhibited those elements which characterized urban problems in American cities: Its racially separated schools provided a focal point for the prejudices and fears of the majority; white families were pulling out, taking with them support for public education; poverty, unemployment, substandard housing and inadequate public services condemned its ghetto to a cycle of defeat; hostility and fear between blacks and whites held the potential for alienation and violence; and, above all, the failure of its public schools to meet the needs of black children foreshadowed an exacerbation of those problems that the past twenty-five years have borne out.

Each program, each function at Westside evolved in response to a serious and immediate need. Most important, those needs had been articulated by staff and supporters of Westside, not by some experts' social and economic surveys. On the simplest level, Westside succeeded because of its ability to communicate those failings of urban education to Pasadena citizens and, at times, to poverty program bureaucrats.

Westside demonstrated that community control depended upon community caring and community self-help. Therefore, change in urban education was possible without massive intervention, without multi-million dollar programs and swarms of highly paid experts. "The culture of poverty," "education for the disadvantaged," or "The War on Poverty" made little sense at Westside. If teachers cared enough to teach, if school officials cared enough to insist on equal education—in other words, if white racism were neutralized—children would learn in city schools.

Westside's educational program proved those simple facts. Its tutoring program, its job training program, and its adult education program all succeeded because of self-help, community concern, and caring. The "hope factor" restored to individuals their dignity, potential and self-esteem. The conclusions for the field of urban studies were so elementary that it was unlikely they would be recognized by economic and social experts whose reputations and livelihoods rested on complex solutions for complex problems.

The founders of Westside knew from their personal experiences in schools that children, especially boys, reached a confrontation point around third or fourth grade. At that point, the humiliation and defeat of not being able to read and write began to have very personal and racial meaning. In the school years that followed, de facto illiteracy meant failure in most other subjects. By young adulthood, that humiliation made necessary either aggression, defeat, or an elaborate pattern of self-deception. Most high school graduates in poverty areas could not read beyond the fifth-grade level.

Students who knew they were bright and capable and wanted to become doctors, lawyers, or electricians also knew the bitter truth—they could not read. Malcolm X's experience was not unusual—he entered jail unable to read a newspaper. Compounding that tragedy, most black parents believed that schools *were* educating their children. They wanted their children to read and write because they had lacked that opportunity. Children in that double bind were programmed for bitterness and aggression. It was typical that the brightest boys set trash fires in the schools, broke windows, and cut classes.

The immediate need Westside served in its tutorial program was for remedial reading and math, as well as assistance with English and grammar. Most importantly, Westside developed an incentive to learn in an environment that was supportive, informal and relaxed. The tutoring program grew—sometimes a class of forty to fifty met in a nine-by-twelve-foot room. Parents became involved. They formed a carpool, organized a crafts program, and provided cookies and juice on Saturdays.

Soon Westside added remedial reading courses and tutorial assistance in math, social studies, and English. Classes were scheduled four evenings a week. Weekends were devoted to craft and recreational activities. A "junior executive" class was conducted on Sundays. The class was specially directed toward those youth with leadership qualities who might otherwise devote time, effort and ingenuity to antisocial activities. To make such a leader useful at Westside was the first step in helping him become useful in society. By the summer of 1966, 200 children and youth were enrolled in the various tutoring programs.

As residents in Northwest Pasadena gained trust in Westside's tutoring services, they turned to the Center for job training and job development. A 1967 survey of the area around Westside revealed that more than four in ten adults had not completed high school; two in ten had not completed more than an eighth grade education. There was an obvious desire for self-improvement: Nearly half of those surveyed indicated a "strong interest" in participating in adult vocational educational programs if such became available. Among those already employed, a substantial interest was expressed in opportunities for job and career advancement if training programs became available (*Community Redev. Agency of Pasadena*).

Westside's approaches in tutoring and job counseling were similar whatever one's age or experience: relate on a one-to-one basis, build trust and self-confidence and the "The Hope Factor." Soon Westside incorporated adult basic education, sensitivity training (both for employers and employees) and vocational training.

The essential step in transforming a hard-core, poverty-bound person into a productive worker was to develop in him a positive attitude and self-image. He had to see himself as a potentially capable and useful member of society. He had to learn to express that new viewpoint so that he could communicate with others. Only then would he have the motivation and adaptability for learning skills and habits that could contribute to employment and advancement in skill levels.

We used the mirror technique and weekly counseling sessions to introduce and support these changes. Often the best counselors were those young men and women who recently had found their own way from street life to useful employment. They were bilingual—could speak both the language of the street and the language of middle-class employers. The counselors dealt with transportation and living problems for first-time job holders. Then, we provided whatever basic skills education was needed to keep the job and progress.

The job training was coordinated with real job openings. Many programs proceeded on an ad hoc basis and then were not repeated. For example, some volunteers from the State Highway Division offered instruction to pass a California exam for Engineering Aides because they had some openings at that time.

In November of 1967, Westside prepared a comprehensive program for adult education called Late Start. We began with semiskilled or unskilled workers who attended classes for five hours each week in order to pass the high school equivalency degree or G.E.D. Westside gave a scholarship of $75 for anyone who successfully finished eight weeks of instruction. In most cases, the money was needed for transportation, babysitting costs or books.

On one end of the job spectrum, unemployed workers with few skills studied basic education along with employment counseling with the goal of finding a job that wasn't a dead end. On the other end of the spectrum, a Caltech professor came in and taught a course in "communication improvement for emerging professionals."

Similarly, some of the adult education was devoted to the difficult task of teaching reading and simple arithmetic to functional illiterates. Yet another component provided advanced tutoring for job advancement in electronics, mathematics or engineering. When workers lacked a particular skill or training, specialized tutoring enabled them to gain a promotion and find a more satisfactory career.

Westside's weekly Community Forum best illustrated its impact in adult education. Each week from fifty to 200 local community residents, Pasadena businessmen, and Caltech professors and students gathered at Westside to hear lectures and panel discussions. The topics ranged from job opportunities, African history and black power to the American Nazi Party, the John Birch Society, and drug abuse. The Community Forum offered poor people an exposure to ideas and personalities important to their lives that newspapers and television rarely afforded.

There was no simple way to add up and assess the effect and value of Westside Study Center's educational programs. The entire operation for tutoring, job training, and adult education cost less than a small elementary school's nonteaching staff. By any test of cost–benefit ratio, the Center brought an enormous return for its budget. But that criterion was almost meaningless. Since both tutors and tutees came voluntarily, both individuals must have benefitted from their sessions. The social gain from each hard-core poverty youth who found counsel and training for a job more than matched the cost of a staff member's salary for a year.

Responding to the failures of Pasadena schools, Westside never developed into a total school system. Westside kept fewer children occupied during the school week than did the public school, but then no truancy laws made anyone come to the Center. Likewise, Westside could not show a regular advance of classes from year to year in national tests for reading and arithmetic. But then Westside's visitors had already been turned off or declared a failure by the schools. If Duke did not find enough of a chance at Westside, the Center at least gave him a better opportunity than had the public schools.

In simplest terms, Westside succeeded because people wanted to come. No better test for schools could be devised. A curriculum centered on the students' needs and desire for knowledge might avoid the task of enforcing truancy laws. Westside Study Center presented a nonhostile, nonfrightening atmosphere. Noise, disorder and difficult questions did not become reasons for disliking kids. Although many tutees first came to find help in passing an exam in the schools, many continued coming because they enjoyed learning. For tutors and adults, Westside provided an opportunity to learn in their own way.

Westside Study Center was a community self-help organization directed toward innovative responses to the failures of urban education. The Center existed only because of the failure of Pasadena to provide equal housing, education, community services and job opportunities for its black citizens. De facto segregation in the schools, combined with inadequate facilities and indifferent teachers and administrators, left black children without the skills and the self-confidence to compete in Pasadena. Racism and failure to deal constructively with urban problems were not unique to Pasadena. On the contrary, Pasadena resembled many medium-sized American cities in its political, social and educational structures.

While the Westside Study Center developed its programs in Northwest Pasadena, the federal government launched its War on Poverty based on community action and "maximum feasible participation" of the poor. After the Watts uprising, in the face of increased political pressure, the War on Poverty's concept of community action came more to resemble community inaction and riot prevention. Westside demonstrated that self-help and community caring were more successful and less contradictory than the War on Poverty's so-called community action.

During this time, Westside Study Center developed extensive programs in child education, job training and job development, and adult literacy. In each program, interaction on a one-to-one basis, establishing trust and self-confidence, and the New Careers concept of upward mobility were basic ingredients. The Center broadened its base of support as its programs for "disadvantaged" blacks in the community attracted the support and participation of many white students, educators, businessmen, and politicians in Pasadena at large.

The key to Westside Study Center's impact in Pasadena was in providing the "The Hope Factor." Westside convinced both those in and out of power, both the advantaged and the disadvantaged, that they could realize their potential and become change agents in their society. The success of the "The Hope Factor" in Westside Study Center's programs suggests new alternatives for black youth, gangs, and urban education.

chapter four

The Boyz (and Girls) in the 'Hood

❏ ❏ ❏

In 1968 I left California and came to the University of Massachusetts in Amherst to teach and complete my doctorate in urban education. I returned to the Los Angeles area in the Fall of 1991, while on faculty sabbatical leave from the University. My goal was to interview gang members and former gang members. Those interviews are the heart of this book and the focus of this chapter.

By 1991, Westside Study Center no longer existed. Washington's War on Poverty had ended in much the same muddle of victory/defeat as the War in Vietnam. Although the Cold War was over, unprecedented levels of gang and police violence in American cities mocked the triumph of peace over Communism's "Evil Empire."

I wanted to see and hear how things had changed since my days at Westside, and how they had stayed the same. Others had interviewed gang members and written about gang life, but I was interested in hearing about their attitudes toward and experiences in school. I wanted to learn about their motivations in joining gangs in order to relate those motivations to education.

Numerous other investigators have focused on the violence of gang life; and you cannot ignore the significance of that violence in youthful lives. Rival shootings and run-ins with the police place gang youth in constant danger, outside the mainstream of social boundaries—even further outside than they already are because they are minority and poor.

Part of the American Dream is the belief/myth that education can lift anyone out of poverty. How does that dream appear to gang members today? From their personal stories, I wanted to find out how gang members' school experiences related to their life histories. Furthermore, I wanted to record how they viewed their schooling looking back in time. At the end of the interview, I asked gang members individually how they would live their life differently if they had it to do over.

In the Pasadena/Altadena area and in Oakland, California, I interviewed present and former gang leaders of the Crips and the Bloods and also talked with girls affiliated with gang members. Their stories are presented in this chapter. I also talked with gang members on probation in Los Angeles County at Pace School. Their stories are part of the following chapter.

In comparing my years at Westside Study Center with today, I saw right away that young people in the 1960s had more hope. They felt they could break out of the mold if someone just gave them a chance: "Where is the door and how can I get through it?" Now, times are much tougher—the jobs are fewer and the consequences of dropping out of school are more deadly.

What *is* the same is that youth still want that chance; they just don't have as much belief in it. Most young black men I talked to wanted to change their lives, but they might not say it directly. One of the hardest things for black males to do is to show weaknesses. Why? They believe that most people are not going to help them. In school, when adults find out your weakness, they log it and use it against you: take your name and send you to the dumb class. So, black young men don't share how they feel easily. Westside Study Center broke through that defensiveness in the 1960s and developed hope. I went back to Westside's area to see if hope is still alive.

The young men I interviewed for this chapter usually said very little about their schooling at first beyond, "It was O.K." or "I did O.K." I asked them if they could remember the names of any teachers from elementary school; most could not. That told me more than their words about how little their teachers helped them. Later in the interview, the young men tended to open up more and say what they might have wanted to go differently for them.

There is a sad irony here: When we started Westside, it was just before the Watts riots, and our slogan was "Time Is Running Out." If we did not do something about education and jobs . . . well, the Watts uprising fulfilled the prophecy. Now, twenty-six years later in Fall of 1991, I went to Southern California to interview street youth, and less than six months later came the Los Angeles uprising in response to the Rodney King verdict. If time was running out in 1965, what is it doing now?

The situation for black youth is worse now all over the country. Working-class jobs have disappeared for everyone. Jobs that young black men used to get have moved to third world countries or been automated. In inner cities, half of the young black men are without jobs. We need to realize *everybody* is an American. Black youth see themselves as Americans. We have to find a way to let them believe they are part of that process. We cannot lock them out of everything, as they now know they're locked out. They see no hope. No chance to work their way up. Gang members say someone has "broken out" to signify moving up to the middle class, as if leaving the ghetto is like escaping from prison.

The times today are much more violent. Kids don't supply the guns which have ever-increasing firepower; but they use them, at younger and younger ages. Another big difference I saw is the attitudes and ways of the police. In the days of Westside, cops would walk into the Center: neighborhood police, probation officers, youth detention camp officers. We had a relationship with all law enforcement in the city. Now, the police only travel in cars and they're moving fast. In some cities, the gangs have more firepower than the police. In a nation with 67 million guns in private hands, it is estimated that 100,000 gang members are armed in Los Angeles County, alone. In 1991, The Centers for Disease Control reported that 1 in 20 teenagers said they brought a gun to school during the previous month. We have created a police state, and we should not have that in America.

In the 1960s California was building the best public school system in the country. It did not always serve black children well. The system was not going to give too much help to a minority child, but the schools had more space and resources. Today, Californians were shocked to learn that their fourth-graders scored next to last on a national reading test (only ahead of Mississippi). California taxpayers are refusing to pay more for education. The state is going broke. Enrollments are up by 30 percent, and minorities make up the majority. In Los Angeles Unified School District, non-Hispanic whites are only 13 percent of enrollment. Hispanic students out-number blacks four to one. Los Angeles teaches children in more than eighty languages! The schools are barely coping. (In 51 of the largest cities in this country, blacks, Hispanics and other minorities are more than half the school-age population.) California is a picture of what the nation in general will look like by 2050. "There is no prosperity in California in the 1990s unless minorities pros-per," said a Palo Alto demographer (*USA Today*, December 4, 1992; *Newsweek*, October 11, 1993).

Youth join gangs when they are locked out of everything else. When you ask them why they join, they mention brotherhood, like a football team, esprit de corps, protection, power. The gang is their family. In black church organizations, the reason for all those deacons and boards is so that people can join, have a role, and work their way up in a system. For these kids, there ought to be some other system in which to work their way up rather than gangs. As a thirty-three year veteran Chicago teacher, who changed the lives of many of his students, puts it: "All those positive things to get you involved and keep you involved, we lack those today. We just don't have the funds for it. And kids are getting involved in gangs . . . because they don't have anything else to do" (*Time,* October 5, 1992).

When we talk about youth and gangs, we have to put it in perspective. First, the majority of black youth are staying in school, not dropping out. Second, the majority are not in trouble with the law and are not in gangs. Furthermore, when we look at white youth from the same socioeconomic conditions, we find similar rates of serious problems—or even higher rates, for example, of hard drug use and violent crimes (Gibbs 1988). The commission that investigated the 1992 L.A. riots found that the gangs were not deeply implicated in the drug organizations. They are not the ones making the big money, nor are they the ones supplying the Uzis. Maybe the gang truce called after the 1992 Los Angeles riots offers an opportunity to involve gang members in rebuilding the city and in positive leadership.

I am not trying to justify or glorify gangs, but to communicate why the young men I talked to felt they had no other alternatives. If I could have Westside Study Center going today, I believe the hardest youth would be doing quite well. If they had a place like that they could belong to, where they could use their skills and build new skills, they wouldn't need the gangs. Above all, they need jobs that lead somewhere, and many would even go on to college.

EX-BLOOD LEADER, DARRYL

Darryl is an ex-Blood leader who has been in the Federal penitentiary. He is about twenty-four years old, a little older than most gang members; you can hear hard experience in his voice. He's out of the gang now and has started his own business with the help of his stepfather. Darryl is tall, over six feet, and extremely nice-looking with a very attractive voice. He looks like his voice, like a movie star.

Darryl's leadership position in the Bloods in Pasadena came from being "the baddest and smartest." He called it "seniority." Sometimes a gang leader will be the guy who lived longest in the projects, but Darryl wasn't from the projects. He lived in Pasadena—not middle-class, but in a nice home with a mother and stepfather who both worked. They helped him when he was in jail and later when he got out. They didn't have much money, but they helped him get started in his own business.

Atron: Tell me a little about yourself in school from grades K through 3. Did you like school? Did you find it interesting?

Darryl: School for me was fun as far as PE and playing around. As far as academics, it was something I didn't excel in.

A: Where did you find the most academic trouble?

D: Third grade, 4th . . . by the 6th grade, I knew how to bullshit the system. If I didn't know a word, if I didn't know a math problem, I knew how to get around it by the 6th grade, and teachers didn't really detect it. There was one teacher that tried to help me, but you know, one teacher doesn't follow you through your whole school years.

A: Do you remember any teachers' names?

D: A few of them, yeah. I went to Altadena Elementary School, and one teacher took an interest in me from 4th to 6th grade: Mr. Morrison, a 6th grade teacher. He saw that by the time I got to his class I knew how to buck the system, but he had only one year to work with me. From there I went to junior high. But some of the things he taught me I still remember today.

A: So, how was junior high school for you?

D: Seventh and 8th grade were just two years that I fought my way through. They were very violent years for me. I stabbed a boy in 7th grade. I went to jail in 7th grade. I didn't learn nothin'. I started to be attractive; girls became a factor. It was girls and violence, 7th and 8th grade; I didn't learn a thing.

High school, the first year was pretty much the same thing. Less violence, but my violence turned from the students towards the teachers. I was more resentful because of what I didn't know. I wasn't high school material.

A: Why did you perceive yourself as being "not high school material?"

D: Well because of 7th and 8th grade, I wasn't prepared for high school. The only year I probably learned anything was in 6th grade and just bits and pieces throughout my younger years. Today, if I had to sit down and write a letter to someone even of a high school level, it wouldn't be adequate.

A: If you had a chance to do it all over again, what would you do to make a difference?

D: If I had a chance to do it all over again, I would be less resentful. I would be easier to deal with. I would be more patient. I didn't have patience with myself. I always thought I was smarter than the teachers. When I didn't learn something as fast as they wanted me to, I thought they were stupid.

A: Do you have any ideas about how we can treat some of the problems of black males in America today?

D: Yeah, I have a lot of ideas, being a black business owner. I served time in Federal prison for being a hard head. I learned in there, for a black man coming out, there's nothing for you. I tried to get a job, but it's no, no, no. Because, it's not what you know, it's who you know. If you've been locked up, who do you know? My family helped me—I had a break. So I was able to make a change for myself. Now I am becoming a reputable black business man, a source in my field. Now, I can focus on hiring my young brothers.

A: You said you went out to talk to (former NFL athlete) Jim Brown about his program?

D: Yes. AmerICAN. He helps ex-gang members try to find jobs. Crips, Bloods, Pirus, from any gangs, they all meet up at his house and talk about solving their problems. So I went to hire one or two to help me in my business.

A: Education hasn't served young men like yourself very well.

D: This is my opinion. It hasn't served black young men well because of the family structure. Once you're in the classroom, it's up to you to get the knowledge. But you can't get the knowledge if you are from a disrupted family.

The older white generation, the people in power, look at a young, black man as a gang member because that's what they see on the media and that's what they read in the paper. Even if you've broken out and are wearing a three-piece suit, they're still going to peg you as a gang member. That's as far as you go. The reason for killing us off. I think genocide is happening now for young black males in America. Nobody's going to prison for it, because it's blacks killing blacks. It's scary.

A: Where are people getting all these guns from?

D: Anyone can get guns. You open up a gun magazine and there's all these automatic weapons. You can get them through the mail. Who's controlling that? Drugs and weapons go hand in hand. The top man supplies the dealers with the weapons. They kill off each other. I know, because I was there. Police have a lot to do with the drugs. They *are* the dope. The war on drugs is for show. Set up a task force for one area. Just for the media. A crack house used to be down here and they moved it. The police know these places exist.

A: Any little neighborhood kid knows it. One mamma told me her child said when she asked him to go on up to the store for some bread, "Not now, Mama, the dealers are on the corner. I'll go later." A little kid ought not to have to deal with that in his neighborhood.

D: The parents know too. If the parents would do something about it, the police would have to react.

A: Back to education: How can we get more young black men going to college?

D: I think we need elementary black academies, just like the black colleges, set up for black kids bonding instead of hurting each other. And we need black teachers. Part of the problem is, like when I was coming up, the white teachers' attitude was just to pass you on, I just want my check.

A: Is Pasadena more middle class now?

D: I think now, the rich are getting richer; some of the middle class have moved up. That's where the majority of Pasadena are going. But a lot of the blacks are just barely making it, being pushed down. Can't afford the new housing. But there are opportunities for minority businesses, a very few.

A: Do you wish you had gone to college?

D: Definitely, not so much for the education but for the contacts. If I didn't learn what I was supposed to learn in my younger years, why would I learn it in college?

A: How did you develop that belief that you couldn't do well?

D: Well, I think a good tool to teach a young kid is to remove the fear of failing. I think my problem always was I was scared not to know a word, or this letter, so I faked it. I was scared to say I didn't know. I was afraid of being made fun of.

A: You'd rather fight than be embarrassed? Isn't that a trait of young black males in school?

D: That's why through my younger years I did a lot of fighting. I was expelled and suspended. I took my frustrations out that way. I was a little bigger than the other kids and faster, so I used that. In my home, there wasn't a whole lot of book learning, but common sense. And that's what's gotten me through my life, just plain old common sense.

A: I would want to see a young man like you get through school with help to get past your deficiencies. You have all these skills you don't even know you have.

D: I think the way to do that is to let a young kid know it's O.K. not to know something. It's O.K. to be slower than your friend. And make the learning process fun, not so intense. For me, it was very intense. It was no fun.

A: Some people are saying black boys ought to be going to school with black male teachers.

D: I think that would be just fine, if they aren't trying to make little soldiers out of these kids. A lot of black families don't have a male figure, and a student can get a balance at school if there isn't a father at home. I think in a different kind of schooling I could have been a good student and would have gone to college. I just want to add, to our younger black men, if we aren't going to excel in books, let's learn a trade and excel in that.

Commentary

Darryl is a good example to explore first. He had the support of a good home. He was an appealing and attractive little boy. But he still failed in school and dealt with that failure with violence and frustration. His experience demonstrates the confrontation point for black kids in the third or fourth grade when they begin being tested and are labelled inadequate. Darryl said he began to "con the system." Why did he have to con the system? They could have taught him. He had nobody to help him except one sixth grade teacher, when it was just about too late.

Let me explain again. He wasn't "conning the system"; he was trying to survive. He knew that if he revealed his weaknesses, he would end up in the dumb room. All black boys know that. They put you there and let you cook potatoes. I remember when I was in fourth grade, one of my buddies said, "Atron, come on and join me in the dumb room. It's fun. We get to cook." Altadena in the 1970s was a little more subtle. They would just track you out of the mainstream. My point is, why give the tests without the treatment plan? Teach the kids and then use the tests to diagnose where to teach more.

Why does Darryl blame the black family structure for kids failing in schools? Quite probably because, like everyone else, he listens to the media. Black kids watch T.V. In one survey of teenage black fathers, each one said that *he* was devoted to his baby and his girlfriend, but all the other teen fathers he knew were irresponsible (Gibbs 1988). They listen to the media. Black youth try not to see themselves as black, but as Americans. If you see yourself as black, you can't break out. Everything is bad, evil. People get caught up in that rhetoric, especially middle-class blacks. Blacks are perceived as the Americans nobody wants.

Toward the end of the interview what Darryl and I were really talking about was love. The most important reform for schools isn't "back to basics." Schooling is still an awful thing for too many children—either because of racism or classism. Some little black boys in school realize nobody is ever going to love them. They learn the lessons of hate. Darryl is well-spoken, attractive to most people, and dignified. As a kid he was bigger and more athletic, but slower at academics. He had to fight for survival and dignity. Other little black boys, less physically appealing or poorer, didn't stand a chance of anyone loving them in school.

CRIP LEADER, JOHN

John is quite different from Darryl—younger, maybe nineteen or twenty, big, heavy-set and looking more like a stereotypical gang member. We met at his grandmother's house where he lived and, because his grandmother was at home, we went outside and talked in his car. John is a Crip leader from Altadena who is getting older and getting smarter about moving beyond the gang scene now. His grandmother wasn't too aware of his activities. My understanding from him is that he wants to go back to school and become a mechanic. If you get that old in the gang business, you get pretty smart. You've been shot at a few times.

John is interesting because he has a foot in both worlds. He lives with his grandmother and takes care of the house and yard for her. He's good to her, helping out and asking, "Grandma, is there anything I can do for you?" But John doesn't have much going for him, because he is kind of an outcast. He looked the gang role—big and threatening. But he could be a gentle giant to his grandmother.

The first story John told me was from a few years back when he got caught in a shooting and almost didn't survive.

John: I'll never again do something that stupid! I was driving, with my brother-in-law's sister next to me, going down to get something to eat. At an intersection, being young and stupid, I gave off a gang sign and flicked 'em off. Next thing I know, I'm being boxed in by three cars, one on each side and one in back of me. The light turned red and a kid got out and just started unloading on me with a thirty-two automatic. Only way out was straight ahead. From then on, I said, "Never again. Too fast for me. I'm still young and I still have a whole young life to live." Now, I listen to my elders who have been in similar problems and understand where they're coming from.

Atron: How did you first get into gangs?

J: Just by hanging out. Right now, some of the old crowd might pull up and say, "What's up, Blood?" But now I'm just home, working on my car. Or fixing up the yard and the house, 'cause now I'm the man of the house. But times have changed. My grandma was telling about this little boy that stole money from his grandmother. I would whup his ass and tell him, "You should be helping your grandma!" Those are the ones that have no parents and no values. Maybe they have a roof over their head, but no guidance.

The kids get into gangs when they say, "How can I be like you?" They watch someone else with a big car and a big sound system and want it too. I asked myself, "How did I get in this predicament?" It was from watching someone else.

A: Do the young kids know that they might die? That when you shoot somebody they might shoot back?

J: They don't care. Around here, they either go to jail or get killed. Like, some cats that I've been to school with, they did what you call "a jack move." They go out of town, say to Huntington, and fake buying from a dealer and rob him instead. And nine times out of ten they'll pull that trigger, 'cause you don't want him coming back after you. Shot in cold blood.

There's no big guys around here any more. No Mafia. Just gangs. No organization or nothing. I could be a Blood and you could be a Crip, yet we grew up together. And I hate you now, because of what you are.

A: Can you be neutral, not belong to a gang?

J: You can stay out, just mind your own business. Like now, I can go any direction, I don't get bothered. Mind my own business. Don't stare anyone down—no "mad-dogging."

A: Do you have any ideas how to motivate the next generation?

J: Myself, I'd like to use a movie camera. Show different ways of life. Do you want this life? Or this life? Home, school, the street, business, all those environments. Who do you see working? Other minorities? Why don't you see many blacks working?

A: How do we get blacks to pull together? Because you're just an American. How do you reach young people in the face of genocide when the enemy is yourself? What you're really saying then is "I don't like me. There's no hope."

J: Well, one problem I have is that middle-class brothers are afraid of me. I think, "Why do you look at me like that? I'm not going to bite you. I'm way beyond thinking about robbing you." But my generation is saying, "I'm starving; I'm broke." The ones that never made it at anything, all they know is how to sell dope or kill somebody. Don't know how to work. Don't know how to read or write or do math.

A: Right now, for them there are no jobs and no hope. Society lets them kill each other off. My question is how do we stop killing off a whole generation of young black men?

J: I myself was sometimes in the wrong place at the wrong time, but I never got caught in a police sweep. I'm going back to school, mechanic school, because anything you want you can get as long as you have an education.

Commentary

John's gotten older in the gang and lost his enthusiasm for going to war. He's been lucky and avoided jail. He's saying that younger kids are more vicious now, more dangerous. And he talks about the loss of respect for grandparents. He escaped being addicted. Most gang members don't do dope and have no respect for junkies. John might survive and get that education as a mechanic. Nobody is going to beat up or "jump out" John. He is a big dude, and known to take care of business. But he has common sense and was getting out. He could do well in a conventional setting. In suburbia they might make him police chief!

PASADENA BLOOD LEADER, RAY

This is a young man who starts out in our interview talking in two-word sentences and then by the end really gets rolling. He's a big kid and a leader. I don't know his age, but he's been out of school for a while. He has a lot to say about how "times have changed."

Atron: How was school for you between kindergarten and third and fourth grade? Do you remember anything about it?

Ray: No, man. I don't know nothin' about it.

A: Did you do well in school?

R: I probably did pretty good to about the sixth grade. Then, I started hangin'.

A: How was junior high school?

R: Junior high? It was all right. Go to school. Started hangin out with gangs in eighth or ninth grade.

A: When did you drop out?

R: About 11th.

A: You stayed a long time.

R: Yeah.

A: Where did you go during the school day?

R: I'd get some weed, sell it. Go to school. Get some more weed. Sell it. And hang out with my boys. Whoever was rolling. Get you an ounce for only $50 and roll up 100 joints. Make some money, that's all.

A: Were you Crip or Red?

R: I was Blood. It's just a neighborhood thing. Claim your set wherever your hood is.

A: Were the Crips and Bloods all black?

R: Whatever people are in the neighborhood—different backgrounds, white, Asian, Hispanic, whoever you are.

A: Were you involved in gang stuff like shootings?

R: Yeah, man, drive-by. Try to be fly—wanna-be. Try to be hard. I don't know if I shot somebody. Poppin' caps, I wasn't hanging around.

A: Anybody shoot back at you?

R: There's always shooting, man. Just got to keep your piece in your lap, that's all. People come through the 'hood rolling, and you're on the corner; got to make some money, brothers just start popping, that's all.

A: I see you've been out of school awhile. If you had it to do all over, would you rather be in school than hang with the boys? Have a house and a car and be a part of the American dream?

R: Yeah, I want all that. I'd like to have all that. Man, the white man ain't gonna let you get too far up there. I just try to do the best I can. Live the life, man. Make the money the best way I can.

A: How long do you think you're going to live if you stay in the gang?

R: I ain't really in the gang no more. I don't really hang. I try to stay at the house now. Niggers are crazy out there, man. I just try to kick it in the house, you know. Too old for that shit now, man.

A: What would you tell younger brothers in the gangs now if you could tell them anything?

R: I'd tell them to get an education and try to stay in school. I know I wish I would have, because I'd probably be doing better than I am now. I try to tell them brothers anyway, but they don't want to listen to me. They're out there making their money, rollin', O.G. ["original gangster"]. I've got younger brothers and cousins, they sell their route and make their money and they don't want to talk about it.

A: What kind of future do you see for young black men, and even whites in the gang, Hispanics or Asians? How many other gangs are there besides the Bloods and Crips?

R: All kinds of gangs. You got Pirus, Bloods, Crips, 1–2–3s, Lady Rus, 4–5–6s, Black Caucus, White Fips, AB Whites, and Chicanos— they're Crips and Bloods just like everybody else. You don't have to be black to claim, just got to live in the 'hood.

A: What about the police?

R: Pasadena police? They ain't shit. They're almost scared, too. They're more worried about themselves, now. They go out two or three in a car. I don't want to deal with a black police and a white police, 'cause the black police will kick your ass to show off for the white cop. That's why the M-F's will be shooting at the cops, man. Cops don't want to talk to young boys no more. Rough you up and put you in the jail house. Now the police are scared. Everybody's packing. Everybody's selling that rock.

    I think it's time for somebody to do something, because the shit's getting out of hand, man. Brothers killing each other. I'm tired of seeing it, man. I wish there was more that I could do personally. Somebody needs to do something. Little kids getting killed on the street. That shit don't need to be happening, man. That's crazy.

Commentary

It seems like a contradiction: members say they got into the gangs looking up to the older boys. But then, when they try to tell younger brothers and cousins to leave it alone, the younger kids don't listen to them. But you have to remember that people need something to believe in—boy scouts, brotherhood, something. So they join. And once they become hard core gang members, in the early stages, they're the most dangerous ones. When you get older, you think about how you might want to survive a little longer. When the young gang members buy their cemetery plots and hang the number around their neck, they aren't planning to live past twenty-one. But you begin to think differently as you approach that age. You might want to survive.

The older gang members I talked to find the younger kids scary today. The power of the weapons is much higher now. It's not a knife or a Saturday night special handgun. Kids have Uzis and semi-automatic weapons that have only one purpose: to kill a lot of people at once. So, it's both that the kids I talked to are older, and ready to get out of gang life, and that the weapons have changed so that it's crazier and more dangerous now.

ALTADENA, CRIP GIRLS

I talked to two tenth-grade girls in Altadena at the home of one of them. They are friends with the Crips. They had a lot to say about gang life, motivations and some drive-by shootings they knew about. They also had strong opinions about "stupid and smart black kids."

When I first began the interview, there were also two boys at the house. The first boy, "Sam," talked to me. He had been to jail for selling dope and now, at eighteen, was trying to get back into school, he said. He looked much younger than eighteen. The second boy wasn't going to talk to me or anyone. I knew better than to try. He was hard; his eyes were "dead."

The first girl, I'll call "Crystal," lives in the house with her mother who is divorced—a hard-working, church-going, strict mother. Crystal's mother keeps track of her and tries to keep track of her associates also. Crystal is very smart, good in school, attractive, and probably will go to college as she says she plans to do. "Janet" is staying at the house with Crystal. She is also very bright and pretty. She stays with Crystal when her grandmother locks her out of the house, which apparently happens often.

I asked Sam if he could tell me anything about his early years in elementary school:

Sam: I did all right. Yes, I remember my 3rd and 4th grade teachers.

Atron: Are you a senior now?

S: I'm in 12th grade, but I'm trying to get back into school. It's hard because I'm eighteen. I didn't drop out. I went to jail for selling dope. I went to CDC school. Then I turned eighteen after I got out. And most schools don't accept you if you're that old.

A: How did you get in a gang?

S: We grew up with each other. Most of Altadena is the Crips, and Pasadena is the Bloods.

A: What are the ages of the gang members?

S: Twelve years old to thirty-five years old.

A: Why do people want to belong?

S: It's like family. A sense of power. Makes them somebody. It's the way you live. Gang members are your role models. All you got to live up to. An O.G. makin money—doesn't have any job. Just on the street selling drugs.

A: If people had opportunities—the hope factor—would they go back to school?

S: Yes, but it depends on how deep you are into it.

[At this point, the girls join the conversation.]

Crystal: I'll say it like this. Most people to me are dumb to be in gangs.

S: To get back in school, they need an incentive, a job.

A: We're incarcerating or killing a whole generation of young black men. How do we stop that cycle?

S: You got to dig deep. You have to collaborate with some other people.

A: What about the younger kids? The next generation up?

S: You got to give them something positive to look forward to.

A: This is what I'm trying to pursue. What is the nature of gangs?

S: It's like a family.

A: But doesn't everyone have a family?

S: No. They got problems at home with their family. Parents might be on dope. Or a father might be beating him, and he don't like him. In a gang, you are somebody. You got some respect.

A: How do you work up the ladder?

S: Put in your work. Shoot somebody. Kill somebody. The older you get, the more work you put in, become an O.G.

A: When is the best time to reach kids?

S: When they are little, yes, 3rd or 4th grade.

Janet: I don't know how to get kids from gangs back in school. If school is not interesting to them, they are not going to go back.
[Both boys leave, and the girls first discuss the two boys.]

C: The other one, he's about seventeen. I do know he's not in school. He's quite sneaky. You can't trust him.

J: It's like, if you do something to him, he's going to get you back. He has a real bad temper.

[Janet talked about her situation. Her brother is in jail and most of her male relatives are in gangs.]

J: For the last four years, I stayed at my father's house, or my mother's and my grandmother's house. If I didn't come home early enough, my grandmother locked me out, and if my mama wasn't there to let me in, I came here. Nearly all my relatives are gang members. My brother went to jail before for selling drugs. Now he's in jail because he wasn't in school and he was driving a car he wasn't supposed to and was running from the police. In sixth grade, that's when it seemed like he was getting in trouble, started hanging with a gang.

C: I had a friend from across the street. He was into gangs and from eleven to seventeen was in and out of jail the whole time. But he's really smart. He would go to summer school and take 9th and 10th grade classes and pass all of those classes—get As and Bs. Most gang members are smarter than regular kids. But he flunked in the regular school.

J: When we were living with my dad, my brother was making better grades than I was. But out here, he was cutting school and getting Fs and I was doing better. I think it was because he changed his friends.

A: How do you two survive and not get hooked up with all this?

C: When I was in the 6th grade, that was my worst year—kickin' with all the boys. I was a tomboy. I stayed out late at night. If my cousin Mya hadn't slowed me down, by now I wouldn't even care about going to school. I have good respect for my mom. I know that if I don't pass all my grades, I'm not gonna get anywhere in life. I'll be pregnant and on welfare by eighteen. A lot of black people to me, now, they're *stupid*. Now that they *can* get somewhere in life, they don't want to do it. Yes, like he said, the gangs are their family. But what they don't realize, they're killing off their own color.

J: It's like, if there's a party up there, you know they're gonna have guns. That's why I don't go. I want my life.

Later, I met with the girls again, and they described a shoot-out near by, one that came to involve them, too. The first incident was after a party when some kids were at a Tastee-Freeze:

Crystal: We heard that Franklin had been shot dead by Bloods. His brother said he was shot twice, but wasn't dead. But the police said he was dead because they thought he and his family would be in danger if he was known to be alive. The next day, Franklin came down here and we saw him.

Janet: There was another time, about six of the Crips were in Blood territory. First, they were parked over here that afternoon, a bunch of sixteen or seventeen year olds, drinking 40s. We kicked it for a long time and went back and forth to the store. Then they heard that a homeboy got shot. They were mad, almost crying, and went off into Bloods' territory that night. One of the boys pulled out a gun and started shooting. The police chased them and caught two of them. The others were running away. After that, three of them came back over here that night.

C: The police caught up to us the next day, because our telephone numbers were on their beepers. They asked us twenty questions. They freaked out my mom. The police said, "This is where the Crips hang out, and your family is in danger." But it wasn't nothin' like that. They weren't kickin' it over here every day. They were just all relatives and homies.

If you see them, you might think they are just gangsters. But it's different if you talk to them. Like, Lionel, he's almost eighteen and he's back in school. He's always telling us "you need to go to school." And he says, "I'm going to settle down soon, get a car." And another one says, "If you stick with me, we aren't ever going back to jail. We aren't getting in any more trouble."

Atron: So how can those boys break out of gang life?

J: If they can see homeboys doing something else—having a job—then they're going to do it too.

Commentary

Crystal lives in a stable situation with a mother and aunt that look after her. She said "So and so can come over, but not so and so unless I tell my mom." But both girls are playing with fire, as the police said, by hanging out with Crips. If they're lucky, they'll get through and probably go to college.

One obvious difference between Altadena/Pasadena of twenty-five years ago and today is the presence of gang violence everywhere. A girl like Crystal, doing well in school, with a hard-working mother keeping track of her, wouldn't have those dangers years ago—dealing with gang members and talking about shoot-outs. I really felt sympathy for her mother and what she faces.

The girls told me that the gang members are often the smarter boys in school, but once they joing a gang, it's hard to get out of that life. There was a story on television last year about a seventy year old Hispanic man who set up a boxing gym in a former county jail in Los Angeles. It took him seven years of working with the kids in the gym to break up the gangs in his community. It's hard to get out of that life. There's nothing to draw them out of it. But at Westside, I had three or four gangs working together. And the gangs broke up right away. It's not easy, but it can be done, especially when the youth themselves help make it happen.

Crystal said the kids will change only if they see their friends change. The homies stick together. There's a story written by a high school junior that tells about the evolution of gangs and the way they can be counteracted. This boy had moved to a tough urban school in Brooklyn, N.Y., for three months and after leaving wrote a story about what he called "The Ducks vs. Hard Rocks." The Ducks are the minority of the minority, the suckers who go to school every day and even want to go to college. The majority are the Hard Rocks. He wrote, "I guess the barrier between the ducks and the hard rocks is the barrier of despair. The ducks still have hope, while the hard rocks are frustrated. They're caught in the deadly, dead-end environment and can't see a way out." He said that the only way to help the hard rocks would be if the ducks could succeed. But the problem is, if they succeed, they tend to feel they don't owe anyone anything: Their attitude is "Let the hard rocks and the junkies stay where they are." The hard rocks want revenge because they have lost all hope: "Their teachers don't offer it, their parents have lost theirs, and their grandparents died with a heartful of hope but nothing to show for it." That teenager pretty much saw the big picture: "Maybe the only people left with hope are the only people who can make a difference—teens like me. We, the ducks, must learn to care. As a fifteen-year-old, I'm not sure I can handle all that" (*Newsweek*, August 18, 1980).

OAKLAND CRIP LEADER, KAHLIL

I went up to Oakland to interview a Crip leader. Kahlil has a low voice, sounds and looks older. He's big and bad—a weight-lifter. His age is somewhere between eighteen and twenty. His hair is cut close, and he has a scar on his face. This is a believable gangster. Oakland is a tough city. He didn't have anybody. This youth was raised in a rough situation. I put his story last. It's the most discouraging. I wish it were the only one like it.

Atron: What was your experience in your early schooling? Do you remember any teachers from then?

Kahlil: I don't remember a whole bunch about that stuff. I only remember one teacher, Mrs. Kelly. But the only reason I remember her is because she hit me. Some kids got on my case, and she hit me with a ruler after the fight. I didn't appreciate that stuff.

A: Tell me a little bit about junior high school.

K: I didn't like it at all. I couldn't read very well. So I just didn't show up for class a lot.

A: Where did you hang?

K: Over at friends' houses and stuff like that. Or down in the canyon.

A: Did you finish? How far did you go?

K: I almost finished tenth grade. I dropped out in tenth grade. Then I went back and tried to finish. But it just wasn't my thing any more.

A: When did you join the gangs?

K: Well, I started hanging out with the guys in fifth grade. But I didn't know it was a gang. We just hung out together. It was fun. These were people I could talk to and I had a good time with them. And I hung out with them from fifth grade past tenth grade. That's really about it.

A: What's the symbol hanging around your neck?

K: This? . . . That's just my thing.

A: What's it for?

K: It's . . . my a . . . my death plot thing. What happened was when I was thirteen, a couple of older guys took me down to this place and got me a plot, so if anything happens to me, I know I'll be buried. That's what it is.

A: I hear you. I know you might not want to talk about that. Are you saying you don't think you'll live very long?

K: The way things go and stuff, you might be here today and might not be here tomorrow.

A: Have you been shot at, involved in terminations?

K: I've heard about things. I don't really want to go into that too deeply. I've been shot at, hit. I've done time.

A: Would you say what for?

K: They claimed that I burglarized some places.

A: I've heard that the young brothers do most of the killings. Is that true?

K: Well, . . . look, basically you got to protect your turf. And you do what you do in order to protect your turf. Yeah, the bottom line is yes. There are kids out there.

A: How old are kids when they start to shoot at people?

K: Well, I had a gun when I was eleven. And I know of other people younger than that. The youngest I heard about taking somebody out was seven.

A: I understand you guys franchise your product a bit.

K: Yeah. . . . Listen, I didn't graduate from high school. So I can't really get a job. The only job I was able to get was a dishwashing job. That didn't even support me at all. Like I didn't have a place to stay. So, like my buddies help me out. And now I have a place of my own and stuff like that. And, it's just a way of life. That's all there is to it.

A: If you had it to do all over again, would you try to be a more traditional kind of person—try to have a car and house and family?

K: Well, yeah. I'd like to wear a three-piece suit and carry a briefcase. You see people walking down the street looking like that, and I wonder where they're going. I wouldn't mind having some sort of a job where I was somebody. I'd like to have a car and stuff like that. Yeah, I want those things, but so what?

A: Could you get out of the life style that you are in now?

K: Nah. Not now.

A: Because, you know you might get killed.

K: Yeah. Everybody "might get killed."

A: Do you think that you'll live to be twenty-one?

K: I never think about it. Not at all.

A: What are some of things that we could do now to help kids in school, people like yourself, so that you would have a better shot? You're a smart person.

K: I still can't read too well.

A: But I understand you are a high-ranking person. I don't think you got there by being stupid.

K: I might be high ranking . . . let's just say I know a few people.

A: If you could do something for young black kids, what would you do?

K: Uh . . . uh. . . . If somebody had cared about me, maybe things might have been a little bit different. I might be able to read a little bit better, maybe. But, nobody took any time out. I don't remember any of my teachers taking any time out. They didn't help me do anything. That's really about it. I think people ought to take time out with their kids. The mother and father. . . . My dad left. I don't know where my mom is now.

A: Did she finish school?

K: She went to school until fifth grade.

A: Anything else you want to share?

K: Uh, no . . . no.

Commentary

The other gang members I talked to could have moved right into conventional society, gone off to college. But Kahlil is really an old man at age twenty. This interview was the saddest and most frightening. He was intelligent. He answered my questions carefully, like a lawyer: "I heard about that," instead of "I saw or I did that." He had nobody. No father, and he doesn't even know where his mother is now. The only teacher he remembers hit him with a ruler. He said it was too late for him: "I'm not going to change now."

All the young men I spoke with wanted better alternatives for their lives. Every one would rather be in school. They just didn't see any reachable alternatives available to them. One fourteen year old said, "I really didn't plan to be in the gang, and I'm glad my younger brother says he isn't going to join." But the reality is that his older brother is in jail at age seventeen with a seven-year term; and he, at fourteen, has already been charged with assault. How much chance is there that his younger brother really won't join the gang? Most urban youth agreed: "The gangs are what's here. There aren't really any other choices."

chapter five

Pace School,
Los Angeles County

❏ ❏ ❏

At Los Angeles County's Pace School, two special groups of young people are helping themselves by helping each other. Lynn Pace School is, first of all, a special education school for multiply handicapped youth from ages three to twenty-two. The CDC (Community Day Centers) schools of Los Angeles County are responsible for educating juvenile offenders after their release from detention facilities or youth camps. At the CDC's, teen offenders on probation perform community service and go to school in a transition period before returning to regular schools or graduating. At Pace School, these two groups in need—youngsters with severe handicaps and juvenile offenders who have served their time—are brought together in a unique program of hope and education. The young people from Southeast CDC have volunteered for a challenging experience: For their community service and as part of their schooling, they teach handicapped children basic skills. This demanding and rewarding work is a part of their school day. Their CDC teachers provide high school courses and assign homework within the setting of their work with the handicapped. For many of them, this is the first useful, positive and successful work they have ever done. Their self-esteem grows enormously. In their academic classes, they find new interest and motivation, often for the first time in their lives, that derives from their success in helping handicapped students.

In the fall of 1991, I went to visit Pace/Southeast because it was one of the rare examples of "The Hope Factor" in action in urban education, utilizing the fundamental strategies that we had found worked at Westside Study Center. It was a school that was doing something to change the lives of young people who had been in gangs, who had gone to jail, who had given up on school, and who had just about given up hope. For the handicapped children and youth, the CDC students changed their lives as well. They received the extra personal attention and emotional commitment that they needed to progress in learning skills and to have hope that their lives, too, could have more meaning. Handicapped adolescents especially needed the opportunity to interact with able-bodied peers, not just adult helpers.

Both groups, of different ages, different races and backgrounds, and different levels of handicaps, see themselves as left out of regular American society. The street kids have been in trouble with teachers, parents and the police since they hit junior high school or before. The handicapped kids can't communicate, move or achieve learning skills like able-bodied students, so they have been left out and put away also. The two groups working together give each other love, accomplishment and self-esteem.

Building self-esteem was the key to "The Hope Factor" at Westside Study Center. When people have hope, there's almost no limit to what they can achieve. In a negative setting, the only lessons learned are negative ones. But how can we jump-start higher self-esteem for youth in gangs or in jail who have long since dropped out of the regular academic process? As they themselves admit, they're past fitting into regular school and achieving traditional academic success. Yet, every gang member or ex-gang member I talked to would rather be in school; that is, they would rather have made it straight if they could have.

The way to jump-start higher self-esteem is through the positive feedback of useful work, especially in helping someone you empathize with. As we will see, the CDC youth working at Pace didn't think at first that they *could* help handicapped children or that they could relate to them. Gradually, in one example after another, those juvenile offenders on probation discovered that they had special gifts and abilities to reach handicapped children. They, too, knew what it felt like to be rejected, to be unable to communicate. They, too, knew how it felt to need more love and attention. They developed patience, responsibility and empathy; and in that process, they developed higher self-esteem.

Useful work is the key to that self-esteem. Many minority and poor youth who have not been successful in school are without viable alternatives in work either. It's a vicious cycle of low self-esteem feeding into gangs and sometimes violence. The best shortcut to raising self-esteem and becoming motivated to pursue an education is to do useful work. And that work means more when it involves the basic human impulse to help someone else.

A University of Massachusetts graduate, Mimi Silbert, discovered that fundamental truth about "helping" work and self-esteem when she founded one of the most successful drug rehabilitation programs in the country, Delancey Street in San Francisco. While working as a therapist and counselor in the early 1970s, she realized that people were thanking her a lot—students, clients, police trainees—and that those thanks provided the basic motivation and nourishment for her work. "And then one day it stuck me—who wants to be the person that has to say thank you all the time? Who wants to be just the receiver?" From that time on at her clinic, every client had the responsibility for helping another client in some practical way. "So that one guy who was a teacher was tutoring a kind of ghetto kid from Oakland. And the kid from Oakland, who was a kind of be-bop artist, I had teaching the very withdrawn sort of child how to dance. And so on and on." The foundation of Delancey Street, then, was developing self-reliance, and the foundation of self-reliance was the higher self-esteem that came from helping others in a practical, useful way (UMass Alumni publication, *Massachusetts* 3,2 Winter 1992).

This was the model that worked at Westside and that I observed again in action at Pace School. Real work, useful work, especially when it is helping others who need you, creates positive feedback. A future emerges. Self-esteem emerges. And with this hope can come the motivation to get an education or training for work in mainstream society.

PACE, A BRIEF HISTORY

The partnership between Pace School for Special Education and the Southeast Community Day Center (CDC), a Juvenile Court and Community School, was the first of its kind in the nation. The program, first conceived by special education director Sharon Roberts, was launched in October 1988 by the Los Angeles County Office of Education. Pace serves two at-risk student populations: the severely handicapped, and high-risk, hard-to-reach youth. Approximately 225 Pace students from ages three to twenty-two include the trainable retarded, multi-handicapped, autistic, and deaf/blind. About thirty to thirty-four youth, ages eleven to seventeen from the Southeast CDC, volunteer to work and study at the school. Most of the students are on probation for a variety of charges including gang activity, substance abuse, weapons, robbery and truancy.

For two hours each morning the CDC students work alongside special education teachers and instructional aides to help administer lessons or tasks to the handicapped. The instruction is individualized and presented in a peer-tutoring style. For their work at Pace, CDC students earn credits toward graduation. In addition to working with the special education students, they can choose other work experience such as office work, health services, and building maintenance.

The Pace and Southeast CDC partnership offers a "least restrictive" environment for at-risk youth whose learning needs are not adequately served through traditional public schools. The school-within-a-school concept provides an opportunity for severely handicapped students to interact and build friendships with able-bodied peers. Two full-time CDC teachers and a half-time aide take primary responsibility for the education and counseling of the CDC youth. Before students can go to their work duties, the teachers check their homework. Later in the day, they meet for regular classes, to which they bring renewed motivation, largely derived from their morning's work.

For the high-risk CDC students, involvement in the program has greatly boosted their self-esteem. Because the peer tutoring is performed in small groups or on an individual basis under the supervision of a special education teacher, the teachers serve as coaches or counselors. Thus, the students are viewed as responsible adults. Their contributions to the learning of the handicapped are genuine and they know it. The result is more positive behavior and re-engagement with future plans and dreams.

It took Sharon Roberts three years to get the Pace/CDC program started. Of course, the L.A. County authorities were leery of the risks of such a new venture. But bringing these two groups together was a natural fit: "Both groups need love and acceptance. They need to feel good about themselves and the gifts they have been given. Everyone needs to be needed," said Roberts. The students on probation have a chance to receive their education—they are not allowed to attend a regular district school—while doing their community work on campus. But while the CDC students are working off their service hours, they are also interacting with handicapped students who really need them and accept them: "We promote something called unconditional love—love that knows no boundaries," said Roberts. "The special ed kids accept the CDC kids, no questions asked. For some of the CDC kids, many of whom come from gang areas, this is the first time they have been accepted for just being themselves, not for some tough image. For others, this is also the first time they have actually been needed."

For the handicapped children, the partnership gives them a chance to interact with peers. "There have been a couple of kids who will not communicate with us as teachers, but then the CDC kids come in, they're laughing and talking and having a good time. Once I asked a CDC student what they talk about that keeps them laughing. He said, 'Nothing much, just girls, cars and Tiajuana. Kid stuff. . . . ' I thought, 'No wonder they don't want to talk to us.' We're dull to them. They talk kid talk. They relate to one another" (Long Beach *Press-Telegram,* May 1, 1991 B3).

The CDC teachers, Cedric Anderson and Sandy Osborn, work hard each day with their students to provide a balance of guidance, discipline, and hard work with love and encouragement. There are rules—you don't wear gang jackets, belts, caps or colors on the Pace campus. Fourteen gangs are represented among the students. But if the students follow the rules and do their schoolwork, they are treated as respected staff members, working side by side with special education teachers. They help the handicapped students walk, eat, use computers and play. The handicapped students have something to offer the CDC students, and the CDC students have something to give to the handicapped. Said Anderson: "Our [handicapped] kids don't have the mental and physical abilities, but they have great emotional strength. The CDC students are just the opposite. They both have strengths and weaknesses, and they capitalize on that" (*Los Angeles Times*, July 8, 1990 J6).

Pictures speak louder than words, and when you visit Pace or look at photos taken at the school, you see scenes that erase your prejudices. A tough-talking gang member is helping a boy with cerebral palsy practice walking by pushing the wheelchair of another disabled youngster. An autistic boy rides in the basket of a three-wheeled bike pedalled by a CDC teenager: As they take a spin through all the classrooms, the laughing boy blows kisses to everyone, including a kiss on the gang member's arm. In another classroom, CDC teenagers help a young boy practice walking and read to an autistic girl.

A young man trying out a new wheelchair is laughing while a gang member offender helps him. They are touching, smiling: The handicapped youth is black; the gang member is white. A twelve year old black boy is tenderly helping a little black girl in a wheelchair wash her hands. Out on the street, he might have to carry a gun. "Tony" helps take care of "Lisa," who is in a wheelchair and cannot talk. He says he is the only one who can understand her. "She's not feeling very good today," he tells me when I visit the school. In another scene, a former gang member helps an eighteen year old girl with cerebral palsy maneuver her wheelchair—her face is alight with a beautiful smile you would see from any teenager meeting a guy she likes.

Cedric Anderson and Sandy Osborn, the CDC teachers, described the Pace program in an overview:

It's a program where pupils learn humility toward humanity. . . . Under the coordination of the court, school teachers and supervision of the special education teachers, both "at risk" groups learn and develop self-esteem, interpersonal relationships, responsibility and unconditional love—love that knows no boundaries. The special education students accept the court school students, no questions asked. For some of the CDC kids, many of whom come from gang areas and are gang members, they have been accepted for just being themselves, not for some tough image. For others, this is also the first time they have actually been needed.

Sharon Roberts, who had worked in special education for several years and then moved over into juvenile court and community schools, discovered that at-risk youth have some of the same problems that the disabled youth have, however, they have more social problems; many of the disabled youth have some social problems, but more physical and mental limitations. "The two groups so much alike and yet so different demonstrate that we can all succeed if we are given an opportunity. Unfortunately these two groups are viewed with fear or are misunderstood by the community. These youth are looked upon as non-productive members of society."

Both youth groups need love and acceptance. They need to feel good about themselves and the gifts they have been given. Everyone needs to be needed. By placing these two youth groups together they develop personal strength through union. They have learned to accept one another, have established good social relationships and become constructive members of society. The community needs to understand that "at risk" youth and disabled youth have a lot of skills and knowledge to bring to the community. They also want to get an education and work, but someone has to be willing to help them. This program provides that special opportunity because by helping others they help themselves. (Anderson, Roberts, and Osborn. "A Nationally Recognized School Program," L.A. County Office of Education, April 1991)

The CDC students stay at the Pace school site for an average of eighty days, or about one report card period. Some of the students I talked to, however, had stayed longer as they approached graduation, were hired as special education aides, and, in one case, even attended junior college. The CDC students at Pace come from a group who show interest and volunteer to learn about the program. Only one-third of students interested in Pace/Southeast agree to enter the program after learning what is required. There is an enrollment process during which, as Sandy Osborn puts it, "they check us out while we check them out." For most of the students, encouragement and the sense of responsibility offered here are the only positives in their lives, helping them to grow academically and socially.

The primary strategy of the Southeast CDC School is to modify behavior first and then gradually develop academic progress. It is the belief of the staff that you cannot teach unless students act appropriately first. Thus the court school staff identified themselves more as counselors rather than teachers. In this way, staff could work on building pupil self-esteem, responsibility, self-discipline and citizenship. It could subsequently improve their socialization skills with their classmates (many of whom are rival gang members), adults and the handicapped.

Pace/Southeast CDC is not a gang prevention program, but rather a gang intervention program. It provides opportunities for street gang youth to receive some respect and dignity from the larger mainstream culture by helping the handicapped students. These gang members are people, they can care about others, but they must have an opportunity to show they can care.

Nearly three-fourths of all CDC students are active participants in street gangs. A gang can be positive or negative depending on its application. Gangs today are typically associated with drug activity, guns and criminal misbehavior. The strategy of the Southeast CDC was to make all students members of the "CDC Gang," a positive gang association designed to serve others: the handicapped, adults and school staff, their CDC peers and the schools. Rather than hurt others, they help others; rather than be destructive, they become constructive members of society. While students have not necessarily left their gang, the idea is to provide a positive alternative.

The program operates daily, five days a week, throughout the school year. It is thus more effective than a two-week summer program or even weekly counseling sessions. Many of the at-risk students who have learning disabilities themselves are learning more by helping the handicapped students read, write and count. The approach of having severely handicapped and non-handicapped students as team members has increased academics, life skills and employment opportunities for both groups. This component is partially responsible for reducing high-risk indices such as poor academic performance, low self-esteem, truancy and poor social relationships in the classroom and at home.

Both student groups, the handicapped and the CDC students, have discovered that by combining their talents, they can be better mainstreamed into society. As many as 29 percent of the at-risk students have been identified as having learning disabilities. Both populations bring a diversity of cultural experiences, be it ethnicity, handicap or environment, that results in a better awareness and understanding of how similar we all are in our need to be accepted.

A comprehensive student demographic study of Pace/Southeast CDC cooperative program was done from October 1988 through October 1990. The results were based on 118 students who attended Southeast CDC during this time period.

Average daily attendance was almost 90 percent. Typically these students have been excessively truant or dropped out of school. About one-thrid of the students had dropped out or were suspended for poor attendance or inappropriate behavior. Ninety-three percent of the pupils had at least a satisfactory community work experience with the handicapped students. Ninety-seven percent of the CDC pupils kept their community service position with the same special education teacher for at least 80 school days (one report card period). Only two physical assaults between CDC pupils and two possession of a weapon incidents occurred on campus. No incidents of fighting occurred between at-risk and handicapped students. The CDC's academic performances improved during their stay from very poor to above average. These students, who are on the average four years behind their academic peers and earn mostly failing grades, are now learning; and 95 percent have earned at least satisfactory grades. Six months after the students leave the CDC school, 64 percent are still in school or working. The norm is generally 30 percent ("An Innovative Collaborative School Program," Los Angeles County Office of Education, Fall 1990).

The highly successful interaction between handicapped Pace students and the CDC students included: instructional interaction (communications (both oral and non-oral) computers, academics, vocational); peer teaching activities (gross and fine motor activities, perceptual motor activities); community education (community walks, shopping, visiting malls); physical activities (lifting and positioning, adaptive physical education, swimming and playground, and track and field events); life skills (social and interpersonal skills, grooming, organizational skills and technical skills); and functional skills (bedmaking, folding clothes, cooking and gardening). The special education training skills that the CDC students acquire provide a solid foundation for future work in the mental health field. Some will go on to further training at community or four-year colleges.

IN THE STUDENTS' WORDS

I visited Pace school three times: first to meet with the principal and twice more to talk with students and observe their classes. I was struck with how good the CDC students were with the handicapped children and teens. They were upbeat, energetic and patient. They used natural ingenuity to encourage withdrawn or discouraged kids to try something new or difficult. I already mentioned the example of "Tony." He worked with "Lisa," a young teen in a wheelchair who could not speak. He understood her better than anyone else. He told me, "Lisa's not feeling well today. She doesn't want to work." Lisa's mother was elated at the progress Lisa had made working with Tony.

I spoke to the Pace CDC students in a busy classroom, usually in pairs, so the interviews were less private or in depth and are shorter than those in Chapter 4. Nevertheless, the eight students I talked to told me about their previous schooling, how they came to be there, and how their lives were changing.

I first spoke with two young black men, about sixteen years old, whom I'll call Harold and Jerome:

Atron: How did you do in school, grades K through 5?

Harold: Right then, I didn't know. I just went. I guess I kind of enjoyed it. I didn't really care.

A: How were your teachers?

H: I didn't know any. I wasn't doing all that well in school, that's all. I was not just doing all my work. I was too lazy. I got into a lot of fights in 4th grade and 5th grade.

Jerome: I really don't remember too much. Like before the 4th grade, I guess I was doing all right. But from 4th grade on up I wasn't doing too good. I wanted to be with my friends and forget about school.

A: Do you remember any teachers?

J: Not really. My friends and I wanted to be playing around, not doing our work.

H: When I was in elementary I used to fight a lot. And they told me, when you get to junior high that's gonna change a lot, because you will be a 6th grader—smaller than everybody else. So, when I got to junior high, I was too lazy to do my work, and the problem I had was fighting a lot and being rebellious against the teachers. Almost every week I would get into a fight. I wouldn't worry about anything else. No, I didn't like any teachers. Only teacher I liked was 6th grade. She was really strict. Everybody said, that's the bitchiest teacher there was. I had her for math and history. I enjoyed the history because she brought in artifacts. And I enjoyed that stuff.

J: Well, by 5th grade they said if I didn't keep up my work they were going to flunk me. But I finally graduated and went up to junior high school, and I started messing up, started ditching, not going to class.

A: Why? How were your grades?

J: Well, I guess probably they didn't want me no more.

A: When did you drop out?

J: I didn't really drop out. They kicked me out. I started going to different schools. I would try going to different schools. And they would accept me into the school. And I would do well for about two weeks. And then I would start ditchin' again. Going out in the community to parks and with my friends.

A: How did you do from junior high level?

H: The thing is, when I got to around 6th grade, my thing was I would like to fight, I don't know why. I was about twelve or thirteen years old, and all my cousins are from a gang, and so I started claiming that gang and messing around with all that. I went to like three junior highs. I went to one, and I got kicked out in 6th grade. I didn't make it through the whole year. And then I moved with my Mom. And I was going over there, and I was doing the same thing. And around that time, the end of 7th grade, I got into problems with three girls who set me up, and I got put in jail. And after I came out of that, I moved with my Dad. When I got to eighth grade is when I started doing better. I made it through the whole school year. I was still being kind of lazy and things. But I made it through the whole year and went to high school.

J: When I got to junior high? I started really getting into not going to school. I really wouldn't want to go to school. I would go to school and then check into class and then leave. One time they gave me a half day—I had to leave before lunch because I could get into fights at lunch. So, when I would leave at lunch, I would make girls ditch and go eat with the girls. And I was doing, you know, stuff for money, illegal stuff for money. So, I got sent to Camp Scott.

H: How I got here, like I said, at the end of 7th grade I got locked up. When I got out of that they sent me to the CDC during the summer, and that's when I made it through the whole year—8th grade. And then I went back to the CDC again, in the summer, because I needed credits. And then I went back to 9th grade about a year and a half ago. And during the second semester of 9th grade, I got kicked out, and I've been in CDC since then. And I'm trying to get back into school now.

J: When I got out of Camp, the regular school wouldn't accept me. So, I came here, checked it out, had my interview, and I pretty much liked it. And I've been here seven months.

H: When you get out you're on probation. Probation says you got to go here. I'm not on probation any more.

A: How do you feel about it here?

H: When they first told me about this place I said, "No man, that ain't me." But now it's pretty good.

J: I think it's pretty good working with the handicapped. Because you get to know a lot of things about handicapped people.

H: That's my story. I'm trying to get back to regular school right now—girls and guys, more social. This school is pretty good to me. But there's pretty good things at the regular school. Co-ed. Socializing. Here, good things because they get you jobs and get you through it and everything.

A: What about gang problems back in the regular school?

H: Right now, I stopped messing around with gangs around a year ago. I still go out, and if I see people that were enemies I just don't talk to them.

J: Yeah. I still hang around. But it's not like before. I've changed a lot. The thing with me though, I can't really get out of it, cuz it's all my family. Brothers, cousins. Everybody I know are from it. Some of them are not doing anything no more, but it's still backing each other up when things are going on.

A: I know you guys do well, good academic work. You might go to college?

J: Sometimes I think about going to college, but then I just forget about it.

H: I just want to be the first one in my family to graduate from high school. Both of my bigger brothers, none of them finished high school. And they could have but they didn't, so I want to be the first one to graduate. And I want to go to college. I want to start a business.

A: I hear you. I was the first one in my family to graduate from high school.

J: I want to be the first to graduate. All my brothers . . . I have a younger sister . . .

H: They said they're gonna put my diploma in a gold frame!

Next, I spoke with two black young men whom I'll call "Mike" and "Richard."

Mike: I liked school. I did all right till I got in about the 7th grade. Started ditchin.' Hung out with my friends and stuff.

A: How were your grades?

M: They were OK. I was getting Bs and Cs. When I was in elementary I remember Miss Crockett and Miss Harris. Two teachers I liked. When I got to 7th grade, I wasn't doing too good because I wasn't going to class. The teacher that was there, he didn't really do anything. Everybody would walk out of class and go off campus and he just called the office. He didn't really care.

Richard: Up to 7th grade school was real cool. I got average grades, did all right. I didn't really consider dropping out until I got to the 10th grade. That's because my mom was sick. I didn't want to leave her alone in the house, and she wanted me to leave, so I just acted like I was going to school. Before that, I was going to school, regular attendance. It was all right.

A: When did you start hanging in the gangs?

R: (Laughing) I was born into the gangs. Started hanging in elementary school.

M: Yeah, you started early.

A: You two are still very young guys. Tell me how you got to here.

M: I got caught GTA . . . robbery. Attempted murder. I didn't do it. And so I didn't go to camp, I just went to Los———; and the next time they caught me, they called my mother to come pick me up. GTA they dropped that case. And attempted murder they dropped that case; and armed robbery, they didn't drop that, and they put me on probation, gave me 30 days. JAWS. Clean now.

R: I was convicted for attempted murder. I have not been home since 1989. I spent time in Youth Authority Camp. While I was at camp my mother passed away. I was sent here by my probation officer. Yeah, I'm in a foster home. Yeah, it's cool.

A: What people sometimes don't know is that boys also need someone to care about them.

Both: [Quietly] Yeah.

A: What about this program?

M: It's good to me. Better than any other regular school. Get out early and got us a job. I'm working. At 12:30 go to work. Go home at 4:30. I like working with the kids. Wasn't hard for me. First I was with the little kids, no problem. Then with the bigger kids, I was already into it. Used to seeing them. It was cool.

R: I think the program is great. Like for most people out on the street our age feel that they have all the problems in the world. They be coming to this school and find out there are people worse off than them. That kind of opens your eyes. Helps you appreciate the way that you are. It kinda makes you feel needed when you work with the kids.

M: Program is great, but we need more people. Need girls!

My next interview was with a white teenager whom I'll call "Sam."

Atron: Tell me about your education in elementary school.

Sam: I got good grades until 7th grade when I started getting into trouble.

A: What kind of trouble?

S: Well, the first time I was lighting incense, and I threw it at my teacher's desk and it caught fire, and they stuck me for arson. It was an accident. Then CDC school and everything. Then to 8th grade. Adams Middle School. I got kicked out. A kid got caught with a BB gun in school and said he got it from me. So I went back to CDC school. I got kicked out for fighting. Then I went to twenty-four-hour school. Got arrested in January for assault. Beat someone up and they pressed charges. I like this school. It's like other CDC schools, but you get to work with handicapped kids. It does make you think how lucky you really are. But, I want to go to regular school. I get really good grades. I want to go to junior college first. And then be a teacher for handicapped people. Then go to regular college and get my credentials while I'm working.

I spoke next to two Hispanic teenagers whom I'll call "Tony" and "Ramon."

Tony: Well, I started good in school, but when I got to 6th and 7th grade I started messing up. I used to belong to a gang and mess around in it. We stole some cars and we got caught. They gave me home probation. I messed up again. I violated parole two times. They put me on placement. Guess I'm gonna do all right now.

Atron: How do you like this program?

T: It's all right. It's nice. I especially like working with the one I showed you [the handicapped girl, "Lisa"].

Ramon: I never went to school. Ditchin' school—I started when I was little. This is my first school.

A: Really?

R: It's been two years here. I'm waiting to graduate and I'm happy about it. Working with the kids. First it was kinda hard, 'cause you're used to being in the street, acting crazy. Here you have to be responsible. Even if you feel mad you got to show a happy face.

T: Yeah. On the street it's really different. We do a lot of things we're not supposed to do here.

R: This program does a lot of things.

T: It helps you. In a lot of other schools, teachers don't pay attention to you because there's too many kids. Here, it's just little kids and that's why they pay a lot of attention to you.

A: Apparently you have real good teachers, right?

R: The teacher helps us. Cares about us. Says, "What's wrong with you?" I like working.

My last interview was with a black girl, high school age, whom I'll call "Teesha."

Teesha: I was a good student. I used to go to school every day. In the 8th grade, I started getting kicked out of school. I started getting tracked like the other students. By the time I got to the 10th grade, everything was falling apart: I wanted to hang out with my friends, thinking drinking and stuff was the way to go. I didn't want to be with my mother no more. I think I was hanging out with the wrong kind of people. It's like one day I went to sleep and I was an angel and I woke up and I was a devil. I wasn't in a gang. I didn't mind my mother. I use to hang. I just wanted to run my own program. Every time I ran away she used to let me come back. One time I ran away in December and I didn't come back until May. And she had a warrant and turned me in. I went to Las Patrinas. At the juvenile facilities, it showed me it wasn't the way to go. They talked to me any kind of way. I went to a different CDC, not like this program. They didn't push me. I used to call and say I was sick. They didn't care. Didn't make me work. For awhile I thought it was O.K. But then it wasn't. I knew I couldn't go on to graduating like that. So, I decided to transfer to this school. I like this school.

It's fun. I do work. And they encourage me to come to school. I really don't like school. But Sandy started telling me to come to school. And I saw somebody that cared. And she showed me. My mother, she be always out to work. I can't say she's a bad mother. My older sister, she works and takes care of us, and I don't know. I come to school every day now. I look at it now, I come to school for the kids. I like working with the kids. I know all the kids and the kids like me a lot. I come to the school for the kids. I'm going to stay with the program until I graduate.

A: Has it been motivating to see kids with more problems than you?

T: I always think what if that was me? How would I want somebody else to treat me? And that's how I treat the kids. I wouldn't want nobody to pick on me and treat me bad and pick on me bad just because I'm slow at doing things normal. I just look at it, if that was me, what would I do? And as I treat all the other kids, I don't treat one more special than the other one. I treat them all the same.

AN ALTERNATIVE TO GANG LIFE

In articles written about Pace, the students and teachers talk about the realities of gang life on the streets and about the alternative Pace provides. "When they come in, they frown and want to look rough and tough," Sandy Osborn said of the gang members. "When I place them in one of these classes, they come back smiling." The Pace campus gives gang members neutral territory, perhaps the only safe place they experience. "These kids take off their gang hats and gang jackets, and they pick up a spoon to feed a child," Osborn said. "And they use their arms, not their fists to fight, but their arms to hug" (*Washington Post*, November 7, 1990 A3).

Alfred, a Crip from Compton, age sixteen, spoke about how his interaction with his gang changed: "When I first came here, I didn't feel comfortable around the kids, but now I look forward to seeing them a lot. I was used to being a thug on the streets, but now when my home-boys come around and expect me to do that kind of stuff, I tell them I have other things to do." Not only does he now have the courage to break away, he also has made that crucial step of admitting his own emotional needs: "This shows that I can do something. It's the first time I've felt like that. I feel more kind-hearted and stuff than I thought I was and I'm not scared to admit it or nothing" (*New York Times*, February 3, 1990).

Salvador was a member of a Long Beach gang. His probation officer talked about the effect of Pace on the sixteen-year-old: "Salvador was a self-centered, selfish kid who you couldn't drag to the school steps. Now that kid is bringing me straight A's. He has learned humility. He has learned compassion. He has learned responsibility." Salvador himself described what being off the streets in a neutral, safe environment means for him: "Here, people look at you as a person. They don't look at you like someone who is going to steal something from them. When someone looks at me like that, I get mad, and I think, 'Well, if that's the way you think, I'll show you,' because it's easier to prove them right than prove them wrong. The [handicapped] kids, they don't look at us like criminals. That's why we want to come here, because they give us a fresh start. We don't have to prove anything to them. They need us here." Nick, a tough-talking kid new to the program had run-ins with the police before he was fourteen years old. He said he wasn't sure he wanted to stay at Pace. But he wanted to graduate and be able to get a good job to buy a nice car and cool clothes. Besides, he admitted, "I want to change myself. I want to be like I was when I was young" (*Los Angeles Times*, July 8, 1990 J6).

STUDENTS AND STAFF WRITE ABOUT PACE

Besides the self-esteem that comes from helping someone else who needs them, the CDC students at Pace learn compassion for someone whose problems are worse than theirs. That compassion helps break through the callousness and fatalism of gang life. "The world of gangs is a very self-centered one with no regard for life," said Laurie Twainham of the Los Angeles County Office of Education. "This program gives them a totally different outlook regarding [human] life."

Both students and staff at Pace wrote down their impressions of the new cooperative experience ("Our Gift to You" and "Staff Stories" Southeast CDC and Pace School Students and Staff). Special education teachers were at first afraid of gang members helping them work and coming to the school. "A lot of teachers were pretty apprehensive at first, but once the kids learned what to do and could just dive right in, it gave us more time for one-on-one work, which is what we really need," said one of the teachers.

Another teacher wrote:

When Cedric and Sandy first approached me and asked if we would be willing to share our class with Southeast Community Day Center (CDC) students, I was not very enthused about the idea. I wondered if these students would follow directions and if they would be willing to do whatever was asked of them. I wasn't sure if they would be able to understand our students and have the patience necessary to gain their trust. I am very glad that I took the chance and said "Yes." I have found the volunteers to be very caring. After an initial period of adjusting, they have been able to do a lot of interacting with the students in the classroom. The additional individual attention this allows for each student has made a big difference in the quality of care the students enjoy. . . . It is wonderful to see the faces of the children brighten when they see one of their special friends come into the room. It has also been wonderful to see the CDC students grow.

A "behavior management" intern described her no-nonsense expectations and apprehensions:

I never thought it would really get through to them, mentally that is. I thought that these hard headed kids from different backgrounds just didn't care if they even made a difference or not. I really thought they just wanted to put in their time and get out. Some of them did, but something happened along the way with the others. They opened up their medieval thinking minds and cleared a path of long forgotten feelings to their hearts. The CDC kids decided that they could make changes. They really do make a difference. How proud we are to have the CDC program on campus!

Everyone knows that secretaries run institutions, schools especially. We couldn't function without them! So, the changing attitudes of two of the secretaries at Pace are especially significant in describing the atmosphere of the school. One retired, temporary office worker wrote:

Having experienced this wonderful program, I feel that I shall never stop working!! When this CDC program started at Pace School, I couldn't help but wonder what these kids would be like. Were they tough, fresh, abusive, frightening, etc., etc.? I wasn't worried about myself but wondered how they would be with the students on campus. There is nothing different about them. . . . They are just kids wanting to be treated like anybody else and that is just what I did. They love affection and I have plenty of that to give . . . and it's free! They also give affection when they know you are sincere. We have had some of the most wonderful boys working in the office and they are very, very intelligent and I know they will go on to better things. We have had a few disappointments and this has personally affected and hurt me more than I would have imagined. When they returned to see me they were truly embarrassed and apologetic but I still had lots of hugs and kisses for them.

Another secretary wrote:

When I first became aware the Community Day Center (CDC) class was going to open at Pace School, I seriously considered requesting a transfer. I was very apprehensive, uptight and definitely concerned about having convicted felons so close by. What I was actually afraid of was the unknown. I knew nothing about these kids: what they were like; what they might do; how they might react; more importantly, how I would react. I was contemplating bringing my very large, very possessive and very vocal dog to school with me! One of the happiest moments I experienced with these kids, was receiving my first (of many) hugs; what an encirclement of warmth, gentle strength and affection I received. I thrive on my daily dose of hugs (as do the kids). One of the saddest moments for me was when a student who (I thought) had great potential, fell back into the trap, and returned to lockup. I felt very let down and extremely disappointed. I felt as if I had experienced a personal loss. I would like everyone (in the world) to know that these kids are just that, kids: wonderful, caring, considerate, lovable kids who just need to find out for themselves how great they really are.

Of course, not every staff story is a happy one. A Mexican-American teacher wrote: "One bright Pace morning a young CDC student came to my room. He was tall and thin. He combed his hair back and called himself Puppet. We talked about his home boys, what it meant and takes to grow up. I felt I had given him something to think about. Someone brought me a newspaper days later and it said Puppet was killed in some alley for crossing some gang member's name out. 'Que paso, con mi amigo Puppet.' "

Walter Lamp, the Pace principal wrote:

I remember one day I was visiting a class when I noticed a student, Jose, with cerebral palsy and severely disabled, seated in his wheelchair. A few minutes later two CDC students, Salvador and Ashley, came in and walked over to Jose and all three immediately started slapping hands in acknowledgement of their friendship.... Sandy Osborn said, "If an at-risk student could give their arms, legs or voice to a handicapped child, they would do it." I believe it!

A metaphor I would use to describe our two youth groups, the handicapped and CDC students is: Both are like birds with broken wings, but if they can embrace, they can both fly together.

Some of the students are very expressive in their writing about the Pace handicapped; others are very shy. But what comes across from all of them is empathy for the handicapped. Sometimes they fantasize wishful thinking—that their handicapped friends could magically be healed. Larry wrote, "If my class of handicapped students could be normal like me, I would ask them to go places with me and kickback. I would like to take them places where they would enjoy themselves such as the beach and amusement parks. I think they'd have a lot of fun."

Armando was particularly touched by a handicapped young man he identified with:

Anthony is twenty-two years old. Every time I wake up in the morning to go to school I really don't feel like going, but I have to. In the CDC class I am tired and sometimes feel down from personal problems, but when I see Anthony I forget my problems and start thinking about his. He's got it worse than me. My problems are nothing to what's wrong with him. He's almost twenty-three years old and still has to wear a diaper and have someone feed him every day.

At first when I came to Pace School I was scared to even touch them cause they had slobber all over themselves.... To tell the truth, before I came here I'd make fun of handicapped or retarded kids. I thought they were so stupid and funny looking, but it's not their fault. I'm the one who should feel real stupid now.

Meeting Anthony has changed me. I thought to myself that as long as I'm here, I'm going to make Anthony the best I can. Sometimes at night I would think to myself "I wonder what these kids feel inside of themselves? What do they dream about? Are they normal in their dreams or still handicapped?" I wish I knew the answers to these questions. Now everyday I look forward to seeing him. When I help Anthony, he starts laughing. It really makes me feel good inside to see him laugh and to see him and other kids having fun and laughing too.... It really makes you feel like somebody because they need you more than you think.

Learning to care for someone is the first step in changing these students' lives. Even when their empathy slips into fantasy, at least they are learning to care. The next step for them is to distinguish between things that can be changed (truancy, studying in school) and things that can't be changed (permanent handicaps or the death of a parent). The final step toward positive adulthood is doing something appropriate about both kinds of situations.

Carlos wrote about this whole progression:

I was really sad when during community service it was time to feed the kids. One of the kids had never eaten so the doctor had to place a tube in his stomach. The teacher had to pour milk through the tube so that the kid wouldn't die of starvation.

I feel better about myself because I get to work with handicapped people. I like working with them because it is a new experience for me. My favorite Pace student is Billy. He's fourteen years old and is severely handicapped. I like working with Billy because he's quiet and he is easy to feed. He likes it when you push him in his wheelchair.

When I leave this school I want to tell everyone that I was proud of working with handicapped kids. Sometimes when I'm with my homeboys they tell me, "Ha, you're probably as dumb as them." That really gets to me, so I told them that it's fun working with the handicapped and that I also learn a lot of stuff from them, as much as they learn from me.

Rudy also describes the difference between his gang life and his new life at Pace:

Ever since I came to this school my life has really changed. People at this school care about you and you learn to care about them. When I first came here I didn't think I could hang on. I used to gang bang every day because I didn't care about life. I was always high, either on weed or on cocaine, but now I enjoy living because the handicapped children need me and I need them. I never had anyone need me before. Sometimes I feel like lending my eyes or my legs to some of these children so they could see or walk. I never imagined myself in a place like this. . . . I know if I wouldn't have come here, I would probably be in jail. If the children here at Pace could understand me, I would tell them how much I care about them and that I love them. And now when my friends ask me to go to ditching parties I say no, I have someone at school waiting for me.

Two of the CDC students described the special pride of making an empathetic bond with their handicapped students:

One of the best things that has happened to me was when I missed school the first time. When I came back to school, Sophie, my Pace teacher, told me the kid I took care of, Timmy (severely handicapped) wouldn't eat. I would usually feed him everyday, but I guess he got attached to me feeding him. She told me he was throwing his food around and would shut his mouth when they tried to feed him. I guess that made me feel good inside. So when I miss school, I think of who's feeding him?

And Jonathan described a breakthrough: "The children I work with are all in wheelchairs and most of them were non-verbal at first. That was strange because I would talk to them and get no response but I can see something in their eyes or maybe their smile, I don't know, but I can understand the child as if he/she is talking to me. One day one of the non-verbal children spoke to me and she said my name. I think that was my most memorable time in my entire life."

CONCLUSION

The words of the Pace students tell their stories better than I can. A second school like Pace has been started in Los Angeles County. The program is easy to replicate if good teachers can be found. It doesn't cost the system any extra resources. After all, in this country it costs $30,000 to $40,000 to incarcerate a prisoner per year— more than the cost of an Ivy League college. Makes you wonder if just *Trading Places* like Eddie Murphy and Dan Akroyd wouldn't result in better success statistics and cost-effectiveness.

Not all of the Pace students are going to make it out of gangs into mainstream society. A high percentage will. They volunteered for the program, and some of those I interviewed described a schooling history in which things didn't begin to go wrong until junior high school, when peer pressure overcame a good beginning.

Pace shows us how many human resources we lose every time we send a young man or woman to prison instead of to school or to productive work. Think of another movie, "Stand and Deliver," based on the true story of Barrio students in East Los Angeles who passed Advanced Placement exams in mathematics—and no one believed they hadn't cheated. This country needs all the human resources we can find in health care needs and in rebuilding our schools, highways, and hope.

My greatest fear for the future of Pace is that the CDC teachers would burn out. They were doing a phenomenal job! They were on top of everything, but didn't come down too hard on the students. They let them mature and find their own way in a safe, controlled and loving environment. Nevertheless, Pace is part of a huge bureaucracy. You have to cheer every time you see that kind of triumph in the midst of bureaucracy; and you have to fear that sooner or later the system will beat them down. I hope not. I'd like to see every youth probation school in this country pair up students with people who need love and personal attention—elderly, handicapped, retarded, homeless, younger kids without parents.

Ms. Roberts mentioned that the next step for the Pace model would be to try to reach youth before they get in big trouble. I agree. Many of the CDC kids' stories reflected that as soon as they got into junior high school, reached puberty, the streets beat out the schools. We need to have meaningful humanistic experiences in schools at that age that give young people a reason to come to school.

So far, we have mainly focused on changing the lives of individuals. How does a gang member turn his life around? Where in his education process did the failures start? How could it have gone differently? What is "The Hope Factor," and what is its vital role in motivating people to buy into the American dream and see a future that includes them?

The next chapter will explore changing whole institutions. The popular term for this process is "renewal." It's a good term. We don't think of individuals "renewing" their lives so much as "turning a corner." But institutions are behemoth creatures. Like oil tankers, they rarely change course rapidly, unless it's onto the rocks. Renewal is a vital part of the life-cycle of institutions. Here, again, "The Hope Factor" plays its central role. If the Pace School model becomes widespread in the California youth penal system, then we will see both the example of individual lives rescued through "The Hope Factor" and of institutions renewed as well.

chapter six

Institutional Racism and Renewal

❏ ❏ ❏

When I came to the School of Education at the University of Massachusetts in Amherst in fall of 1968, I was drawn by the chance to pursue a doctorate, to teach, and to take part in the revolutionary design—by students and faculty—of a new education school. All would join in a special planning year where the only curriculum would be designing a new school of education. We would construct an institution which would be dedicated to improving public schools, to a world perspective, to respect for all races, sexes, ages and religions, and to educating youth for the twenty-first century.

Nineteen-sixty-eight was a watershed year for this nation. The country was still reeling from the assassination of President Kennedy in 1963, the assassination of Malcolm X in 1965 and the riots in Watts and other major cities that long hot summer, and the escalation of the Vietnam War in 1967 and 1968.

Nineteen-sixty-eight began with the Tet Offensive in Vietnam, a deciding factor in public opinion, along with the My Lai massacre, to bring overwhelming pressure to end the war. In the last year of his administration, President Johnson became a virtual prisoner in the White House because of ubiquitous anti-war protests. He decided against running for a second term. In April of 1968, in the heat of the presidential primaries, Martin Luther King, Jr. was assassinated. Two months later, moments after sewing up the California Democratic primary, presidential candidate Robert Kennedy was assassinated. The Democratic Party Convention that summer in Chicago erupted with police violence against demonstrators that had not been portrayed on television since Police Chief Bull Connor turned fire hoses and attack dogs against civil rights protestors in Birmingham, Alabama, in the early 1960s.

It is impossible to measure the loss to our nation of the four slain leaders: John F. Kennedy, Malcolm X, Martin Luther King, Jr. and Robert F. Kennedy. In the early 1960s, President Kennedy and his Attorney General, Robert Kennedy, were reluctantly dragged into the violent battles in the deep South over civil rights: the integration of Ol' Miss, the freedom rides and sit-ins, and the voter registration crusades. The South had been a traditional bulwark of white, Democratic Party power. In fact, the Baptist minister, Reverend Martin Luther King, Sr. had been opposed to candidate John F. Kennedy at first, because, like many Protestants in this country, he mistrusted a Catholic president. However, when Kennedy sent federal troops to intervene in the violence in Birmingham, a new bond of trust was forged between an American president and African American leaders not seen since the time of Abraham Lincoln.

Malcolm X had been a controversial leader in his years as Minister for the Black Muslims. His separatist message seemed to be opposite that of Reverend King and the integrationists. In the last year of his life, when he was estranged from Elijah Muhammad, Malcolm X visited Egypt, made his pilgrimage to Mecca, and forged a new world vision of his Muslim religion which transcended any kind of racism. There was talk of conciliation between him and Martin Luther King, Jr. before Malcolm X was shot down in 1965.

Reverend Martin Luther King, Jr. may have had his greatest impact on all Americans when he led nonviolent demonstrations in Birmingham, Alabama, against American apartheid. His popular leadership culminated in the March on Washington of 1963 and his now famous "I Have a Dream" speech. At that point in time, King and other civil rights leaders were struggling to carry the movement to the next level of economic equal rights. It was one thing to ask white Americans to guarantee black Americans the rights to vote, to go to integrated public schools, and to travel on public transportation. Support was widespread for those fundamental individual rights. It was another thing to ask white Americans to open the doors of *their* community schools and neighborhoods and to give up occupational advantages to fellow black citizens. At the time of his death, King was embroiled in strategic disputes that continue to this day over how to win equal rights and opportunities in our prejudiced society.

The lost potential leadership of Robert Kennedy was more difficult to measure. During his bid for the Democratic nomination, he showed disillusionment with the Vietnam War, which he had originally supported. In his relationships with civil rights leaders and other black citizens, he was beginning to speak a language of new hope and racial amelioration that the nation desperately needed. When his funeral train traveled from New York to Washington, D.C., thousands gathered to say farewell—in some locations, blacks on one side and whites on the other side of the tracks.

The hopes kindled by the four leaders were not fully realized. After the assassinations, the Nixon presidency collapsed in the disillusionment of Watergate. The Vietnam War ground on for five more years, with the deaths of 25,000 more American soldiers. Thereafter, the tasks of dealing with racial divisions and economic inequities would be much harder to tackle and would proceed at a slower pace without their visions and leadership.

COMBATTING INSTITUTIONAL RACISM

After the planning year concluded at the new School of Education at UMass, the faculty and graduate students went on a weekend retreat to review priorities for the years ahead. They voted that the number one priority of the School of Education would be "combatting institutional racism" in schools, at the university, and in the wider society. In 1970, what did our school mean by the term "institutional racism?" What does it mean today?

Institutional racism does not necessarily require individual acts of prejudice or discrimination to perpetuate past acts and structures of racism. It refers to inequities and prejudices embedded in institutions that will be perpetuated by "business as usual." One example is the culturally biased I.Q. tests referred to in Chapter 2.

If the test items predominantly reflect the knowledge and culture familiar to European-descended, middle-class youngsters, then other groups will be at a disadvantage. The reverse of this can be seen in the general inability of middle-class whites to comprehend street "rap." Using culturally-biased tests to sort diverse students into academic tracks is a prime example of institutional racism. (See Knowles and Prewitt 1969; Hacker 1992).

Another example would be a school curriculum that only transmits a Eurocentric perspective. American history textbooks that ignore the contributions of African or Native Americans convey a message of invisibility to minority students. Why are students not taught that Alexander Hamilton was black, or that the founder of Chicago was a black explorer?

Probably the most blatant examples of institutional racism appear in school and voter districting in cities. Gerrymandered districts can be drawn up by city officials to suit racist agendas. For example, to keep certain schools mostly black and neighboring districts mostly white, district lines can be drawn around housing clusters segregated by race. However, in order to prevent minority voters from achieving proportional representation in municipal government, different lines can be drawn for voting precincts to keep minority representation spread out. Hispanic Americans, for example, could represent 40 percent of the city's population, but have no elected representatives because they represent only 10 percent of various districts. Historically, when cities' redistricting plans failed to prevent minority representation, then moving to at-large (citywide) elections achieved the same outcome.

Traditionally, skilled workers' unions or municipal unions have kept a tight hold on apprenticeships, passing them down like an inheritance, keeping out minorities and women. Applicants would be sorted by examinations unrelated to skills essential to job performance. When a seniority system of "last hired, first fired" is applied, it becomes very difficult for minorities to permanently break into previously all white job pools.

At every level of educational attainment, black men earn 20 to 25 percent less than white counterparts (in recent years, black women have earned much closer to parity). In the highest categories—four years of college and five or more years of college—black male earnings drop off *further* relative to whites (Hacker, 1992).

The strategy of affirmative action was devised to overcome historical institutional racism. It called for actively seeking out minority employees or college-professional students in roughly their proportion within the population. Dating back to the days of President Franklin D. Roosevelt, various federal rules, guidelines or laws sought to combat job discrimination. Some job areas, such as police and fire departments, bank tellers and electricians, have dramatically increased black worker participation in the past twenty years. Others, such as university teaching, have greatly increased participation of women, while failing to significantly increase participation of black men. The bitter conventional wisdom has been, "Women's Rights took a ride on the Civil Rights Movement, and black men are still waiting."

It has been a mixed blessing that a large proportion of black male professionals find work in the public sector. They have been most vulnerable to public budget cuts. For example, between 1979 and 1989, the income of black college men declined 11 percent largely due to a drop in government hiring; while for white college men, income increased 11 percent because the private economy was expanding (Hacker 1992).

Institutional racism is stubborn in its resistance to change. However, an enriched and equal public education for all students could do much to hasten its demise.

THE SINGULAR CASE OF THE AMERICAN MILITARY

Before turning to examples of institutional renewal in the context of education and urban youth, we need to explore the American institution that has had more impact than any other on the lives of young black males: the military services. In his study of black family history, Andrew Billingsley devoted an entire chapter to "The Influence of the Military."

When General Colin Powell, an African American, became Chairman of the Joint Chiefs of Staff in 1989, a breakthrough was achieved in minority career advancement that was more than forty years in the making. President Truman had desegregated the armed forces in 1948. Suspending the draft in 1972, President Nixon decreed an all-volunteer armed services. In the 1970s and

1980s, minorities and women dramatically increased their participation in the military. By 1985, in the army, 10 percent of commissioned officers and one-third of noncommissioned officers were black—a record in minority promotions unequaled anywhere else in American institutions.

Today, the volunteer armed services recruit a high proportion of minorities through the appeal of access to higher education and job training, a reliable salary, and fewer risks of discrimination than are found in other institutions. In 1985, 400,000 black enlistees made up nearly 30 percent of the armed forces. To an amazing extent, the dramatic integration of the armed forces was achieved with intelligent preparation and a minimum of conflict. "The armed forces still have racial problems, but these are minimal compared with the problems that exist in other institutions, public and private" (Billingsley 1992, 194).

Billingsley hypothesized that unlike public schools, universities and housing markets, the military is a "closed system" and a hierarchy. That may account for its success in rapidly desegregating. Certainly, the role of positive and unyielding leadership has been important. When educational, political or community leaders show courage and leadership, dramatic changes can be achieved.

It is ironic that in the recent era of erosion of civil rights, economic backsliding and diminished quality of life in inner cities for poor and minority Americans, the armed forces stand out as the greatest institutional success story of the 1980s. Despite representing the epitome of bureaucracy and hierarchy, the armed forces' quality of personnel, education level and ability to function effectively have never been higher.

In the imminent downsizing of the American military to reap the "peace dividend" after the end of the Cold War, it would be disastrous if African Americans were most heavily impacted. That will happen, however, unless career retraining becomes available for ex-servicemen suddenly without jobs.

LEADERSHIP FOR INSTITUTIONAL RENEWAL

The stories of Westside Study Center (Chapter 3) and of Pace School (Chapter 5) show how individuals can turn their lives around in an atmosphere of hope, through helping others and renewing self-esteem. These examples are crucial to my thesis that even the "hardest" gang members are open to education and positive roles in American society. Teachers and future teachers should know that they can become a part of the solution, not a part of the problem, in providing "The Hope Factor" in urban schools.

Beginning teachers sometimes find themselves in institutional settings so negative and hopeless that they quickly become as discouraged as their students. In this chapter, we offer teachers and future teachers their own "Hope Factor" by identifying at least the minimum basic elements needed in institutional settings for individuals to grow and contribute.

The first large-scale educational restructuring that I took part in at the University of Massachusetts was the federally-funded Career Opportunities Program (COP). This program was designed to meet two needs at once: the need for career lattices and education for urban poor, and the need for more urban classroom teachers whose racial background reflected the diversity of the students in the schools.

By the 1970s, huge urban school districts such as New York City were in turmoil. Immense, unwieldy bureaucracies administered large, centralized districts. Classrooms had become increasingly minority, while teachers had remained overwhelmingly white and middle class. Conflict was inevitable. In the "community control" disputes and a bitter, year-long teachers' strike, racial and ethnic divisions intensified.

The federal COP program was designed to offer teacher aides (paraprofessionals)—usually minority parents or veterans from the community—enhanced roles in the classrooms and an on-site undergraduate program in teacher education. From the School of Education and the wider University of Massachusetts community, faculty and staff traveled to Brooklyn, New York, and Springfield and Worcester, Massachusetts, to offer course work and in-service training to more than 350 paraprofessionals. In the summer, the mostly black and Hispanic teachers-in-training came on campus to UMass to take courses and experience university life. The exposure to new people and new environments was mutually beneficial.

Despite some criticism and political pressures, the federal Career Opportunities Program was a success. Parents and veterans from poor communities received educational and vocational opportunities while bringing balance to the racial, ethnic and economic makeup of school staffing. Where "the stick" approach had failed—in the divisive New York teachers' strike and community control strife—"the carrot" approach could succeed, by creating programs of mutual benefits for schools, community education aides, and universities.

The fundamental elements of COP were the same as those of the Westside Study Center: personal empowerment through service, education and enhanced self-esteem; new lines of communication forged through mutual help among previously polarized groups; and the power of mutually beneficial efforts that combined to renew institutions.

After my first eight years of administering federal and other urban programs at the School of Education, I took a leave of absence to work in the mental health education field in Ohio. At Cleveland Developmental Center our task was to educate for re-entry into the outside world the educable mentally retarded, some of whom had spent most of their lives in institutions. The task called for reforming the entire institution where staff and clients alike had become demoralized in a negative setting. Like many urban schools, staff only went through the motions of helping clients or took their frustrations out on them, feeling as abused by the system as did their clients. The clients had been treated negatively as useless "retards" for so long that they did not know how to behave otherwise.

Furthermore, like the worst urban schools, power and control did not flow in a predictable management chart from the director on down to the humblest worker. Power and control resided hit or miss within the institution depending on access to resources, information and political support (Patterson et al. 1986). The whole institution had to be renewed and provided with "The Hope Factor."

First of all, I changed all of the routines and many of the rules and regulations. Staff were freed up to pursue their own education through various choices and to work in teams for improving working conditions. The clients were now to be considered "students." Each one had a personal educational plan, recorded in his or her own notebook. Staff said to me, "You can't give them their own notebooks! They'll lose them in a day." In more than a year there, I never knew a client ("student") to lose a notebook!

When the staff had more hope in their lives and saw that their work could achieve some positive results, they became more effective and far more supportive. When the "students" began to be treated with dignity, they made tremendous learning and behavior gains which would help prepare them for re-entry into the world outside. Working with the "experts" such as speech pathologists, who before had made no impact in the negative institutional setting, I asked, "Just cure two students!" In other words, take all your professional training and technique and show me some practical results. It was extremely gratifying to me to witness the "awakenings" of both staff and students when "The Hope Factor" and personal empowerment were introduced to a previously moribund institution.

CASE STUDY: BOSTON SECONDARY SCHOOLS PROJECT

When I returned to the School of Education at UMass, Amherst, in 1978, we embarked on an evolving model of institutional renewal for an entire urban educational system: the Boston Secondary Schools Project, or BSSP.[1]

The Boston Secondary Schools Project was a major school-university collaboration, carried on for fifteen years in a large urban system. Conducted jointly by the School of Education, University of Massachusetts, Amherst, and the Boston school system, BSSP began in 1975 in one school, Boston English High School. By 1985, BSSP had grown to include seventeen intermediate and secondary schools, over 125 teachers, staff and principals and more than a dozen university faculty. The project's central and constant purpose was to facilitate school-based improvement efforts.

The accomplishments of the BSSP school improvement strategies took place during recurring upheavals in Boston public schools in the 1970s and 1980s. The Federal Court Desegregation Order of 1974 brought to the public eye the racial separation and ethnic fears and loyalties of Boston that spilled over into anti-busing protest and violence. The Phase II Court Order of 1975 redrew districts, created magnet schools and instituted school-university pairings. The fledgling success of those reforms was sorely tested in 1980–81—the year BSSP expanded to twelve participating schools—when the superintendent was fired, a budget crisis threatened to shut down the schools, 1,000 teachers were to be laid off, a bus strike paralyzed transportation, and a School Committee member was charged with extortion.

In the context of citywide crises and loss of public support for Boston schools, BSSP was undertaken specifically to address school-based reform. Teams of teachers from various disciplines led by school administrators worked with university support and for university credit to remedy such problems as school attendance, high drop out rates, negative school climate, inadequate curriculum, low student achievement, and staff disillusionment.

This model for school-based team collaborative reform confirmed previous school improvement research and pointed towards future school-university partnerships for effective educational renewal. For a close up view of the model, we will turn to two sets of interviews of participants, from 1981 and 1989, and to individual team reports from one exemplary school, Jamaica Plain. Conclusions from the studies, and from related school reform research, provide outlines of the BSSP model and key elements of its success. The words of participants provide a closer look at the process. The *model* is important in order to describe an exemplary school improvement strategy; the *process* is the essence of perceived "success" or "failure" and the model's underlying reality.

BSSP Team Model

The heart of BSSP was a team of teachers from a school working with the active support of the headmaster (principal), in close collaboration with university faculty, with the primary goal of school improvement. An unusual feature of the program was the opportunity for BSSP participants to pursue advanced degrees or credits as part of their school improvement efforts. BSSP degree students—teachers, staff or principals—were members of school improvement teams as part of the requirements of graduate degree programs leading toward a Master of Education, a Certificate of Advanced Graduate Study, or a Doctor of Education. Other students enrolled in BSSP courses as part of their continuing professional development or as part of other degree programs.

The University of Massachusetts, Amherst, Boston Secondary Schools Project began in 1975 with the English High School in Boston. From the original English High Teacher Center, designed to enable staff development and school improvement within Boston's largest high school, the BSSP grew to a network of twelve middle and high schools (later expanded to seventeen). Over fifteen years, 669 educators participated and 115 graduate degrees were awarded. The Project operated with the endorsement and collaborative support of the University President's Office and the University of Massachusetts, Boston, the Boston School Department, Cambridge School Department, and other outlying districts. The Project office, classroom and meeting space were located at the UMass President's office in downtown Boston. In 1979, BSSP received the Distinguished Achievement Award of the American Association of Colleges for Teacher Education. In March 1985, faculty of BSSP were selected to present at the AACTE National Convention in Denver on the topic, "How Teams Work: Considerations of Collaborators."

Team cooperation took place on several levels simultaneously. The school-based BSSP team consisted of the headmaster and participating teachers and staff. They met weekly to solve specific problems within their individual schools and prepared group and individual reports for academic credit. They also took related academic courses taught on site at BSSP headquarters. Participating university faculty, administrators and adjunct faculty, plus consultants, formed another team that met weekly to plan, conduct classes and workshops and visit schools. Finally, a team of principals (team-leaders) met bi-weekly to discuss processes, agendas, problems and potentials for their teams. Once each semester, a "Mini-Sabbatical" brought all these teams together on campus in Amherst, ninety miles away from Boston, for further academic input, reflection and interaction. As the individual interviews attest, these multi-layered teams served both a formal structure in the BSSP design and an informal structure to increase communication, diminish isolation and build trust and camaraderie.

Team Effectiveness Research—BSSP Overview

BSSP was congruent with school improvement concepts from related research on staff development and school improvement (Brookover and Lezotte 1979; Edmonds 1979; Rutter et al. 1979; Comer 1980; Sarason 1982; Boyer 1983; Lightfoot 1983; Goodlad 1984). Those concepts, which constituted the ongoing improvement agenda of the Project were:

- the individual school is the optimal unit for effecting positive change
- any effective school improvement effort requires the active support of the headmaster
- increased opportunity to participate in organizational decision making for teachers can lead to greater productivity and increased capacity for effective action
- collaboration between schools and institutions of higher education, to be effective, requires voluntary participation, shared planning and decision making, a joint problem-solving approach, and recognition that both are complex organizations undergoing changes
- effective collaboration and school improvement efforts depend upon comprehensive and long-term commitments
- university graduate study (courses, research, advising, reflection "time-out," dissertations) serves as a common denominator for participants in the project and provides a forum to articulate the skills and knowledge needed to effect school-based change.

When the new Boston Superintendent, Robert R. Spillane, addressed principals and headmasters in August 1981, he reiterated the basic features of effective schools and his educational philosophy that *all children can learn*. Most important, he envisioned those elements, not as isolated formulas, but as cumulative, interacting factors: "The key ingredients are teamwork and a systematic use of resources. . . . Principals must be held accountable for leading effective educational teams and seeing that the needs of all students are addressed." (Spillane, Robert. Speech to principals, headmasters, and other key personnel, August 26, 1981, West Roxbury High School, Boston, Mass.) The Boston Secondary Schools Project brought such teams to life.

Teams in which individuals from various formal levels take on new informal roles can serve to integrate complex, dynamic reality with a desired positive institutional outcome. Problem-solving teams bring improvement efforts closer to the source of the problem by creating communication and mutual respect where silence and suspicion existed. They address the critical failures of bureaucratic hierarchies to allow communication and empowerment.

Jamaica Plain High School Team

Historically, the Boston School System was a typical intractable bureaucracy operating according to myriad political, social and personal agendas while presenting to the public a systematic hierarchy of place and position. It was an educational system that in 1974 the federal courts judged illegally unresponsive to the needs of minorities and that historically offered few upward avenues for women and minorities working in its system.

In 1980, Jamaica Plain was a high school of 1,100 students that had three headmasters in as many years and that had just moved from its historic, crumbling old "castle" on the hill to a large renovated facility, formerly a factory. The school population was approximately 50 percent black, 33 percent Hispanic, and 17 percent white. The new headmaster, Stacy Johnson, had participated in the BSSP team at Boston English High. In his new role, he was eager to use the BSSP team model to help bring order to the chaos he inherited. Johnson actively recruited a new BSSP team of thirteen members reflecting the diversity of school staff.

The new team included the headmaster as leader, the assistant headmaster, teachers and staff, and the coordinator of the school's court-mandated pairing with Simmons College. In its first year, the Jamaica Plain team struggled, endlessly to some, with setting goals. Johnson directed the process by asking each team member to name three goals that he then listed on the board and asked to be vigorously defended. The UMass consultants introduced the "Key Results Planning Process" borrowed from industrial models that helped members focus on their goals. Basically, ideal outcomes were described (Key Results), and then steps were agreed upon that could lead to those outcomes.

The Jamaica Plain team chose "school climate" as its broad goal for improvement. Then, individual team members took on specific roles. One member directed the organization of the chaotic school student records. Others worked on new policies for lateness, absences and detentions. When some of these small goals began to be reached, other teachers and staff who were not on the BSSP team began to appreciate the school improvements.

The Jamaica Plain BSSP team operated effectively from 1980 through 1985, increasing at one time from one to two teams. In 1981–82, the Key Result sought was improved school climate. In 1983, the team served as the vehicle to prepare for accreditation. In 1984, their focus shifted to curriculum: reading and math. In 1985, they worked on the problem of drop-outs.

Interviews of Jamaica Plain team members in 1981 and again in 1989 provide a close look at the *process* of team functioning both at the time of most challenge and later, in retrospect. Certain themes emerge in almost every interview: for the individual, the issues of time off, access to knowledge and decision making, less isolation, buying into a group commitment, and personal frustration with a new process; for the team as a group, diversity, a broader "holistic" picture, a network and spread of positive results, momentum and synergy of effort, reality-based solutions, collegiality and breaking down of barriers; for the headmaster, learning trust, becoming empowered to effect changes, ending isolation and breaking down barriers.

Jametta Hunt was a school administrator (Housemaster) at Jamaica Plain and served on the first BSSP team in 1980–81, before leaving to move into central administration in Boston. Since she had also served on a team at Boston English, she saw the process in different settings and from the perspective of its early history:

Originally, I really wanted to participate for the *network*. I was skeptical that I would be able to go to the university. I wanted the contact with administrators and the opportunity to have an overview of school operation—to end isolation and share reports. It was like being in a doll house in just one room and then moving outside and visualizing the whole. The team members didn't see before that it was necessary to work together. We were just in our own class and doin' fine.

Ms. Hunt described the fine line of the team leader between guidance and domination: "If the leader dominates too much or sets goals too soon, it won't work. Stacy (Johnson) had to learn to trust the group. They needed to feel ownership for their decisions.

We had some heated meetings about relinquishing power. It was a growing time for him, too." The previous headmasters had met plenty of resistance to change in an atmosphere of chaos and divided loyalties. The team provided a vehicle for change and communication, school wide. "Everyone had their own interest area; through the team you could achieve your interest. It was essential to have the time set aside. Sometimes the long, heated discussions were frustrating, but we felt like pioneers—part of something beyond ourselves!"

At a small staff meeting in 1989, Stacy Johnson and several Jamaica Plain teachers reminisced about the struggles and successes of the first years of the BSSP team. Said Johnson:

Without the team, I never would have gotten the time with those people to make changes and put systems in place. If you go back to the first team at Boston English, it's amazing the number of people who fanned out to new positions in Boston and elsewhere from this program. UMass never got the accolades they deserved from this system. . . . They were involved in almost every major innovation in Boston. As teachers improve themselves, the students are the recipients.

Placida Galdi, a bilingual teacher and department head who participated in the first team said in 1989, "I joined to be with others in the school. We tended to be separate. It was a link to our own teachers. The long discussion process was frustrating, but of great value as department head." Galdi described another benefit of the school-university association: "Once a year the UMass student teachers came here and visited our classrooms. It really motivated us to show off our best. Teachers were openly willing to host students. I was amazed!"

Math teacher Charles Behnke joined the team in its second year. "I had no intention to do it, but Stacy pulled me in. I'm usually skeptical, but I could see what the BSSP team did for the school. We pulled everyone's topics under the umbrella, 'school climate.' Everyone had a vested interest—we were a magnet. The whole was greater than the parts."

Johnson and Behnke described the frustration with the long process of setting goals. "It was very difficult and we *were* frustrated," said Johnson. "We couldn't have done it without Key Results. But the *process* was great; there was receptivity to the necessity to go through with it." Added Behnke, "We did the design faithfully, every other week, at times twice a week. But when a few semesters were over we could see what was chaotic and unstructured becoming structured and accomplished." Johnson summarized: "We began to see the big picture and we collectively *decided* what we wanted to do. We outgrew some of the old ways. We wanted to be people ahead—people carrying weight. At the Mini-Sabbatical, we got to know each other socially too. The biggest thing was, we improved the school for everyone."

Marilyn Corsini, the Assistant Headmaster, remembered the formation of the first team and the impact the process had on her future role:

In the past, evaluating teachers—part of my job—only deteriorated relations with the faculty. The process was demeaning. We had no training—just were told to be leaders. Participating in the team and learning to use the Key Results Plan changed the way I do my job. For the BSSP team, Stacy chose a real cross-section of teachers and administrators. We *all* needed the training together. We shared the highs and lows. I could see a cross-section of talents and strengths emerge. For me, it's the only way now. No administrator can patronize or impose. You can have a great theory from a consultant, but it can stop right at the classroom door without on-going support and activities.

It is revealing to look back eight years to interviews of the same team members and others conducted in 1981 by Geraldine O'Donnell as part of her doctoral research. When Ms. O'Donnell interviewed team members, the expanded BSSP had existed for about one year. Furthermore, the Boston School Department was facing unprecedented crises, summarized in a 1981, *Boston Globe* article: "One thousand of the 4500 teachers are scheduled to be laid off. . . . In the past year, they had three superintendents, a school committeeman-turned extortionist, a three week bus strike, and five months of worrying whether the system would stay open for 180 days" ("Hub School Year Was Touch and Go," June 21, 1981).

The interviews from 1981 reveal more about the risks, dangers and frustrations that were present at the formative stages of what became a very successful team. Bard Hamlen, the Coordinator from Simmons, had been at Jamaica Plain since the 1975 court mandated pairing. She said in 1981:

The team presented different risks for everyone. For many people, it was just academic, raising all those specters of institutional learning . . . and many are nervous in the group situation. For one former administrator, it's a personal risk. I think anyone working in Boston at this point is taking risks. I'm not sure just why people are willing to do it. One variable is Stacy and his optimism—his sense that this school is going to make it. It's a new chance, a new building.

Ms. Hamlen addressed some of the frustrations of team participation: the headmaster may become spread too thin and not be there when you need him; leaders on the team sometimes have to hold back and not dominate; and some members are very hesitant to take *any* risks. "Working in a group, you can only go so far as the most timid member, otherwise you run the risk of losing them and it could debilitate the group."

In 1981, the Assistant Headmaster, Marilyn Corsini, had worked with three different headmasters in three years. She said, "The present headmaster has expectations for the school which are different than the others and this has definitely helped. We have all joined in to buying into his expectations which he shared with the team."

The comments of one original team member, Helen Tyler, a career education counselor, revealed how difficult team dynamics were for someone accustomed to top-down authority. "We really weren't sure what was expected of us." Despite her discomfort, she saw a personal growth: "I have grown tremendously because of my participation. It has allowed me and encouraged me—those are two different processes—to assume leadership which I had not previously assumed." At the same time, she described "personal satisfaction, being part of what you feel as the power structure, and there is a satisfaction in having the support of the headmaster."

Judith Fischer, a Jamaica Plain team member from Simmons College, volunteered an outsider's view of the problems in school climate that the team hoped to address:

These included several changes in headmasters in the past few years, a move to a new school, changes in citywide guidelines, changes in personnel in charge of implementation in various areas, a feeling by some that it was impossible to set up uniform policy and procedures, the feeling by others of not caring, and the feelings of still others that they wished to make sure that things *didn't* work, and that those things that did were destroyed. The result of all of this was very low morale and a feeling of worthlessness, hopelessness and powerlessness on the part of many in the school.

Ms. Fischer noted that although the achievement of Key Results seemed frustratingly slow to some team members, the impact was schoolwide:

The UMass team has made very good progress in implementing its key result. Many procedures, policies and organizational patterns which either didn't exist or were poorly formulated or not uniformly carried out, now are in place. Faculty are slowly beginning to understand these procedures, policies and organizational patterns, and many are beginning to further understand that the implementation of these is not a threat to them, but rather will make their lives a whole lot more pleasant and a great deal easier.

Despite frustrations from lack of time, the greatest value of the team effort, according to Ms. Fischer, was "focusing on the problem, as well as developing a team rapport—the sense of belonging to something to which one is willing to give and willing to take risks."

Bard Hamlen's April 1981 team paper agreed: "Something had certainly happened over the course of the year which enabled us to sense a unity of purpose and comfortableness with one another which hadn't been there in the beginning."

From the perspective of a graduate student in several different institutions, Ms. Hamlen praised the attitudes of BSSP staff and faculty:

Clearly its staff demonstrates an understanding of how to treat adults in an education setting . . . with confidence in and respect for its "students." Such a teacher/student relationship is far too rare in adult education situations in my experience. Academic hurdles, the challenge mentality, the power issue are still too often found in the in-service classroom. Rigidity, condescension, a kind of superiority over the "benighted classroom teacher unaware of new research" is still too common an attitude on the part of in-service educators.

Ms. Hamlen cited an ongoing study of the court-mandated pairings of schools and universities in Boston that concluded that true collaborations were more successful than imposing an outside program. "In my experience a particular problem of Boston Collaborative Programs has been the relatively few number of college/university staff who seem to have the inclination and/or the ability to work constructively with Boston School personnel. Genuine respect for Boston School teachers is one of the basic requirements, one would hope, but it seems a rather rare commodity."

Eight years later in 1989, in an interview of several of the Jamaica Plain team members, Aileen Rice and Bard Hamlen looked at some of the early frustrations in retrospect. Said Rice, "We had quite a critical first report of the team decision-making process." Karen Williams, from the first team, elaborated: "What motivated people to join was input into school improvement. The team provided focus and a way to spread the decision-making process." Bard Hamlen offered her perspective as faculty from another institution: "BSSP offered the most creative practitioner research model— learning and doing, group consensus, collegiality not hierarchy, and a forum which at first is unstructured but then empowers." Betty Carter, also from the first team, said, "I enjoyed most the collegiality and meeting people at other schools. The team process if it's well-structured is useful." In summary, Ms. Hamlen said, "Jamaica Plain has learned how to do this—teams and action. We keep doing it now, without anxiety about it. I always believed it was the way to go. At Jamaica Plain, they institutionalized it."

In his interview in 1989, Charles Behnke summed up the life-cycle of the teams: "When Stacy came, it was a new school and we got off to a rocky start in the school and in the program. Those efforts peaked a year or two ago in terms of improved scores, attendance, school climate, guidance—all those systems. We were pretty proud, and we had fought for our school. For three or four years, it really worked! I was sad to see it go." Stacy Johnson added, "Now, the whole system is pretty deflated. We're still going forward, but through three or four years of pure hell here. What I miss most of all is how *much* it meant for me to have them as a team!"

SCHOOL-UNIVERSITY COLLABORATION

In summary, the Boston Secondary Schools Project brought positive change and school improvement on a wide scale to a system that had become dysfunctional and resistant to outside evaluators as well as change agents. Through a long-term commitment and the medium of school-based problem-solving teams, UMass Amherst faculty were accepted and gained trust and credibility in a system usually inured to taking risks. Headmasters and their staff embarked on new relationships and modes of communication that unearthed fresh approaches to perennial urban education problems.

When the headmasters and team leaders met to discuss BSSP team progress, there was an openness not characteristic of their other official meetings. As Headmaster Stacy Johnson reported, the beneficiaries of such improvements were first and foremost the students. Teachers and administrators also found new ways to make more workable and humane those systems that alienated everyone and accomplished little.

The 1980–81 Boston Secondary Schools Project Report acknowledged both the potential and the problems in designing such mutual commitments:

Neither the revenues nor enrollments generated by this program justify the time and number of university faculty involved. Rather, justification comes from the real expectations for school improvement, for the return of public faith in the effectiveness of urban public high schools, and of the possibilities that the university and Boston Public School personnel can learn together in ways that may help others around the country.

During the late 1960s and 1970s, it became fashionable to blame the victims, citing the shortcomings of the disadvantaged students in urban classrooms. In the 1980s, the blame was often shifted to teachers for "A Nation at Risk." There are signs that in the 1990s, educators may look to changing systems and settings as well as creating collaborations to bring positive change to schools.

Despite the difficulties, as John Goodlad pointed out, "progress with the hard educational problems requires a school-university collaboration.... [T]he responsibilities of these two institutions for improving the quality of schooling are virtually inseparable." Furthermore, elevating the status of teachers requires more than simply increasing required course credits or adding on a master's year of training: "Relationships between production of knowledge and personnel in the field of education and ongoing school practice are sufficiently loose as to make education one of the weakest professions" (Goodlad 1987).

A nationwide consortium of more than ninety university schools of education endorsed a new design of "Professional Development Schools"—universities in partnership with schoolpeople. "A Professional Development School will uniquely combine four functions: clinical preparation of student teachers, inquiry on issues important to the school's practitioners as well as to the university's researchers, the reformation of the school to serve its own student population and community, and the continuing learning of the school's teachers and administrators" (Holmes Group *Forum*, "Tomorrow's Schools," [Winter 1990] 4:2).

For the first time on a large scale, university educators have acknowledged that the future of the education profession lies in collaboration of all concerned. Beginning in 1990–91, the Michigan Partnership for New Education, with $48 million state-corporate-university funding, established eighteen to twenty-four Professional Development Schools around the state.

The success of educational collaboration models in Michigan and elsewhere will have national impact. In the Commonwealth of Massachusetts, fiscal crisis has precluded any other model for educational renewal besides collaboration and cooperation. These models, like BSSP before them, will rely on team cooperation to break down bureaucratic barriers, to diminish professional isolation, to generate new approaches, to turn efforts from assigning blame to effecting real school improvements. This will empower all the players on the stage of education—teachers, administrators, university faculty and students.

Student teachers, interns and beginning teachers have the basic right to expect to work in an institutional setting in which renewal can be an ongoing process for the students, the teachers and the school itself. In their training and internship, they should be exposed to the examples of master teachers in effective schools in a variety of settings with a diversity of race and class. In professional development schools, university teams can work closely with public school teams to improve school conditions, conduct meaningful educational research, and train the next generation of caring and effective teachers.

Institutional renewal is always harder at first than just continuing in the old ways of doing things. Everybody has to "give up" something and yet have faith that the future will be brighter for everybody. To end previous isolation, new lines of communication and cross-fertilization are forged within the planning teams.

As I learned, first at Westside Study Center, then at numerous other educational institutions, the whole can become greater than the sum of its parts. Individuals or power groups need to be convinced that it is in their interest to give up something (power, resources, status) in the short-run for greater gains in the long run. Time and again, that is the basic story of institutional renewal.

NOTE

1. Parts of this chapter appeared in *The Teacher Educator* (1991) 27:2, and in *American Secondary Education* (1992) 20:4

chapter seven

A National Agenda to Save Urban Youth

❏ ❏ ❏

During the 1992 presidential elections, President Bush proclaimed that this generation could now "sleep safely in their beds" because America had won the Cold War. He neglected to mention the inner-city children who are put to bed in bathtubs or in back bedrooms to protect them from stray bullets in street wars. When those children become adolescents, they will face more violence on the street and the added risk that they may be participating in it. The loss of so many young futures to gang violence (there are 100,000 gang members in Los Angeles, alone) is our gravest national crisis. The violence and corruption of the international drug trade—mainlining through inner cities and rapidly spreading to the suburbs—poses as much peril to this nation as the "Red Menace" of Communism conjured up in the 1950s.

Education is not the whole answer to this crisis. But the gang members I interviewed in Chapters 4 and 5 all wished they had stayed in school—even those who said it was too late for them now. As "Kahlil" concluded: "If somebody [in school] had cared about me, things might have been a little bit different. But nobody took any time out."

The studies of problems that beset inner-city teens show the onset of those problems at an early age—from as young as eight or nine years of age. At a conference in Orlando, Florida, on gangs, schools and community that we attended in May 1993, Richard Arthur, a California urban educator for 39 years, had this to say: "I never met a gang kid that wanted to be in a gang! They want what we all want: money, love, success. They get nothing out of school and no support from home. The schools should be helping. Why are they getting kicked out, even in elementary schools and then graduated into prison?"

He asked former gang members before he came to the conference, "What message should I tell people?" They answered: "Tell them to help kids in elementary school. After that, it's too late." Likewise, I asked "Sam" in Altadena, California, "When is the best time to reach kids about gangs?" and he answered: "When they are little, yes, third or fourth grade." Clearly, the problems faced by urban youth *must* be addressed in the context of their schools.

In Chapter 2, we briefly surveyed the major issues of urban education, including race and class, tracking, the confrontation point in elementary school, and issues of power and access for older students. In Chapters 3 and 5 we explored "The Hope Factor" as a strategy for helping oneself through helping others. Meaningful helping roles, like students' work with handicapped children at Pace School, can "jump start" low self-esteem and rescue lost lives almost overnight. In Chapter 6, we examined how "The Hope Factor" could renew institutions as well as individuals.

In this chapter, I want to revisit our basic themes, primarily in the context of education. Above all, I want to communicate a positive message of hope to future teachers—most of whom will work in schools with many minority students—and to those who will train those teachers for the twenty-first century.

A National Agenda to Save Urban Youth is, in fact, a call to improve education for *all* American youth. In this nation, there can be no excellence without equity. Many Americans from all walks of life have lost faith in their institutions. "The Hope Factor" underlies the American Dream, a belief in a positive future for all our children. It is the essential glue of a diverse democracy.

IT'S NOT EASY, BUT WE KNOW ENOUGH

Mobilizing national resources and the political will to rescue urban youth is our top priority. Making fundamental educational changes, however, is never a simple process. We come up against a basic paradox: scientists and educational researchers know very little about how people learn and how the brain actually "works," yet they know enough about human aspirations and motivations to make every school a successful school and to lead every child to reach his or her highest potential.

The first half of this paradox was underlined at a March 1993 symposium at Massachusetts Institute of Technology called "Mind and Media: Rethinking Thinking." Distinguished Professors Seymour Papert (creator of LOGO) and Marvin Minsky lamented how little progress we have made in understanding the learning process in the past twenty-five years—neuro-anatomically, psychologically or educationally. On the other hand, common sense and numerous examples of successful schools in practice continuously provide hope and models for replication.

Analogously, the underlying assumption of scientific research that all problems are potentially solvable is clearly open to question in the context of complex institutions. Seymour Sarason (1982) called for greater awareness of what he called "intractable problems." Instead of "intractable" problems, I would prefer to describe "recurring problems"—the hard work each generation has to undertake anew to raise its children, safeguard individual rights, fulfill individual potential, and create hope.

Improving education in America occurs in a complex, community-based, individualized, often politicized process. After studying thirty-eight schools in thirteen communities—8,624 parents, 1,350 teachers and 17,163 students in seven regions of the country, John Goodlad concluded that, schools differ everywhere, while "schooling" remains much the same. "If we are to improve schooling, we must improve individual schools" (Goodlad 1984). Not a very glamorous prescription, but common sense.

To restate the paradox, then, fundamental assumptions about learning, intelligence, equity and individual potential must be sought, reexamined and restated as part of a national agenda to improve schools. However, implementing changes based on those assumptions will depend on individual communities and vary from school to school. Furthermore, we need not wait for scientific certainty or a "magic bullet" before improving schools. Change is difficult, but we already know enough.

I would like to return to what Andrew Billingsley said about the American military—that more than any other institution it successfully desegregated, probably because it is a "closed system,"unlike public education, which is an "open system." Changes in schools cannot be mandated by a school board or superintendent, or even by a principal acting alone. Public schools represent multiple agendas and what the authors of *Productive School Systems for a Nonrational World* called "nonrational" models of organization. Here are some of the fundamental differences between rational models and nonrational models, or, if you will, between the American military (a closed system) and American public schools (an open system):

The *goals* of a rational model are clear, stable, and set by its leaders; while the goals of a nonrational model are multiple, ambiguous, subject to change, sometimes competing, and arrived at through bargaining among many different forces, both inside and outside the system.

Power in a rational model flows along the same lines as its formal, hierarchical chart, and there is a direct connection in the chain of command between directives and behaviors, from top to bottom. Power in a nonrational model resides throughout the organization, according to access to information, support and resources; and those at the foot soldier level, such as teachers in the classrooms, control the extent to which central office directives are carried out.

Decision making is likewise dramatically different in the military-closed-rational model versus the public schools-open-nonrational model. In the former, the most important issues for the institution receive the most time; all options are considered, extraneous forces from the outside are kept at bay; the external environment shows constraint, support, respect and acknowledges autonomy; and decisions made usually maximize organizational goals. In contrast, in the latter nonrational model, issues most pressing at the time get the most attention, options are usually limited by external factors, extraneous forces are accommodated, external forces demand input at every stage, and the process usually results in compromise and concession not necessarily in the best interests of the institution (Patterson et al. 1986).

In their study of *Partnerships for Improving Schools*, Jones and Maloy described the "multiple realities" (different ways of seeing and experiencing) that can lead to "ill-structured problems" in schools—when something is amiss and no standard procedures seem to work. When teams approach such problems with trust, they can be a very positive force, leading to personal and institutional renewal (Jones and Maloy 1988).

Reiterating our findings for institutional renewal in Chapter 6, cooperating teams, formed ad hoc to solve "ill-structured" problems, can operate successfully within such nonrational models, that is, within public schools, to empower individual students, parents, teachers, staff and administrators. New lines of communication and shared goals ensure that desired changes will be implemented. Such teams will be even more powerful when they make connections to related outside institutions such as universities, businesses, police, courts, health centers and cultural institutions. As our interviews with the teachers at Jamaica Plain High School in Boston revealed, problem-solving in teams is at first more difficult and more time consuming. But the gains in trust, communication and new ways of seeing ultimately outweigh the initial frustrations.

Supporting that strategy, a study of *School Success and Staff Development* by Judith Warren Little identified two very broad and powerful norms observed at unusually successful public schools: *collegiality* among staff and *continuous improvement*, reflecting the expectation that improvements in instruction and performance are continuous, never-ending, and enacted by analysis, evaluation and experimentation with instructional practices.

According to Little, successful school staffs would show:

- frequent *talk* among teachers about teaching, not just about characteristics of students or problems from the community; and

- frequent *observation* of the practice of teaching, including teachers frequently observing each other. The steep learning curves and adaptability of the beginning teacher should last for a career!

In summary, while educators will always keep searching for more understanding of how children learn and how best to enhance that learning, we know enough today to educate every child in America to his or her full potential. Secondly, while we cannot implement changes in schools by a top down directive, a nationally mobilized moral and political will to save urban youth is critical at this point in time. We can make changes in individual schools when we recognize the power of "The Hope Factor" to create new problem-solving teams, new lines of communication, and individual empowerment.

COMMON MIRACLES IN ELEMENTARY SCHOOLS

In Chapter 2 when we discussed issues of education and equity, race and class, we identified the "confrontation point" in elementary school at third or fourth grade when urban children, especially black boys, begin to lose ground and tune out of schools because of the hostility and lack of support they encounter. As "Darryl" phrased it, "I learned to con the system." Most gang members I interviewed did not remember the names of their elementary school teachers, except Kahlil who remembered, "Mrs. Kelly, because she hit me with a ruler."

Of course, the previous years in preschool and kindergarten through fourth grade are vitally important. In those years, as recommended by the Carnegie report, *An Imperiled Generation*, schools should have ungraded, language-rich programs in small, individualized settings, with a minimum of rigid instructional grouping and with parents cooperating as co-teachers.

Preschool programs such as Head Start should be fully funded so that children from all backgrounds have opportunities for enriched educational preparation. The expectations for pre-kindergarten education should be as unbiased as *Sesame Street* and as lofty as Montessori schools. Support for children with emotional or physical deprivations should be coordinated with schools, families and relevant health and social agencies. Yale psychiatrist Dr. James Comer implemented such successful problem-solving support teams for New Haven school children. By coordinating the interventions of school staff, social agencies and parents ("parents are gold"), problems are solved before they become insurmountable (Comer 1980).

The top priority of elementary schools K through fourth should be to teach all children to read. Other countries, even those without homogeneous populations, have proved this can be done. New Zealand has the highest literacy rate in the world. There, elementary schools make learning to read their highest priority. Native Maori children from poor families learn to read alongside middle-class white children. Their daily reading literature is appealing and imaginative. Testing is diagnostic, not punitive. The responsibility for success is placed on the schools, and they deliver.

In the Amherst, Massachusetts, elementary schools, the new "Step Up to Reading" program is modeled on the success of the New Zealand schools. In the earliest grades, children who lag behind in their reading development (about 10 percent of first graders) are given daily tutoring (totalling a half a day per week of individualized help) in order to prevent falling behind their peers. After one year in the program, eighteen of twenty participating first-graders tested as average readers for their age group. To implement this level of commitment, schools that are short on resources could mobilize parents, retired citizens and older students to help in one-on-one tutoring.

For the past six years, some of the poorest elementary schools in Baltimore have been trying out a reading program that provides intensive extra help in the first two grades. Professor Robert Slavin of Johns Hopkins created "Success for All" as an inexpensive, tutor-intensive program to help urban children keep up in developing reading skills. In a given school, all the first grade teachers divide children into reading ability groups and teach them intensively, with extra tutoring time given to those who need it most. Every eight weeks the groups are tested and rearranged. Schools that used this program had children who by the fifth grade were reading at or close to grade level, while children not in the program had fallen a grade or more behind (Winerip 1993).

Elementary schools should be happy, safe environments that nurture each child's positive self-image. It is important that the schools appreciate the cultural differences of all students. Holidays and celebrations have exaggerated importance for elementary school children, and teachers and schools must ensure that everyone's heritage is honored in some way. Teachers need to be sensitive to different family backgrounds of students. It seems obvious in this day and age that classroom activities that assume a child has a traditional nuclear family will deeply hurt those children who live in alternative family settings such as with a grandparent, with a single parent, or in a foster home.

There are other intellectual, social and aesthetic tools that we hope students will master in elementary school: writing, spelling and verbal expression; mathematical reasoning and problem-solving; computer use for word processing and individualized curricular exploration; conflict resolution and group problem-solving; self-expression through the arts and physical education; good sportsmanship and citizenship; appreciation of cultural differences and empathy for others; and awareness of healthy practices. Without success in learning to read, however, children are going to feel inadequate in the world of schools, a world in which they will spend thirteen years either moving successfully from one accomplishment to another, or falling farther and farther behind their peers on the road to eventually dropping out.

The KEEP (Kamehameha) Early Education Program in Hawaii developed and studied a language arts early elementary education program over the past twenty years that began with an exploration of cultural compatibility in elementary classrooms for children of Hawaiian ancestry. They examined school cultures from the eyes of anthropologists. What went on in elementary classrooms, and how were those customs and expectations consonant or dissonant with what went on in a traditional Hawaiian family? They observed, for example, that Hawaiian families greatly valued giving to the family group and putting one's own needs and ego second to the needs and identity of the family. Those values were often in conflict with the mainstream American individualistic values encouraged in the elementary classrooms.

In the typical North American classroom, a teacher assigns tasks to the whole group, followed by some individual practice, followed by individual assessment. That system is not necessarily the most effective for students from all cultures. Teachers assume that a student who does not tune in to that structure is unmotivated, rather than recognizing it may be an alien social organization. The KEEP program designed small independent group tasks rich in peer teaching-learning with the teacher roving from group to group. Hawaiian children's language arts learning dramatically improved. A similar model was introduced for comparison in Northern Arizona Navajo classrooms. However, because Navajo culture clearly separates male and female roles from a young age, only when the peer groups were reorganized as all male and all female did peer assistance become frequent (Tharp 1992).

The street rap of black urban youth reflects the cultural value of rhyme, rhythm and oral improvisation "on stage." From my generation, "Playing the Dozens" was rap's predecessor. Schools should mine this rich cultural vein, not suppress it. Rap, break dancing, younger children's skills at jump-rope rhymes—these all reflect intelligence and creativity that schools could build on, instead of merely trying to "correct" Black English.

Other examples are emerging, as educators pay more attention to the cultures that children bring to school. M. D. Williams' observations of ghetto children in Pittsburgh schools led him to conclude that students' staging of impromptu "dramas" to tease, test, and sometimes intimidate teachers could be transformed from "delinquent" behavior to positive learning modes. Others have explored different story-telling styles of children from different cultures (Tharp 1992).

Another important communication variable is conversational "wait time"—how long someone pauses between listening and responding. A long pause may appear polite to one culture (Japanese), but an embarrassing silence to another (North American). Informal interrupting (overlapping conversation) may be considered friendly by Hawaiian children, but rude to their Anglo teacher. Vietnamese children are taught that it is rude to look adults in the eyes when they address them. Their American teachers may think students are being rude or disobedient if they look down while being addressed.

In another example of capitalizing on culture, in Japan Dr. Shinzuo Suzuki developed a revolutionary method to teach violin to young children that he called "The Mother Tongue Method" and "Talent Education." He observed that all healthy children seemed to learn to speak their native language naturally, through positive interaction with adults. He decided to develop a similar musical instrument curriculum for very young (pre-reader) children. Toddler-aged children learn to talk through a positive interaction, and parents seem to be naturally charmed and pleased by infant and toddler efforts to communicate. As children experiment with language, they receive positive reinforcement from parents and from other children. Seldom do they receive punishment for their mistakes!

Dr. Suzuki's play-by-ear lessons were adapted to provide fun and success for the youngest students, sometimes only two years old. He built tiny violins that progressed to larger ones as the children grew. Parents joined in at every step. He steadfastly held to the theory that every child had musical talent and the ability to learn to play the violin if she learned through love. Many traditional classical instructors were horrified (brainwashing?!) at his methods. Now, they have been adopted worldwide. Children from around the world, some as young as six or seven years old, play violin as competently and joyfully as many adults. The Suzuki revolution in music proved the positive results of high expectations and lessons taught with love.

A few examples of such high expectations for children's accomplishments can be found in American urban classrooms. The Key School in Indianapolis is entirely designed around the belief that children possess many kinds of intelligence. The question for educators to explore is not "How intelligent are you?" but "How are you intelligent?" Like Dr. Suzuki's Talent Education Program, the Key School teachers act upon the assumption that every child is gifted—"and they prove it" (reported on ABC Television News Special: "Common Miracles: The New American Revolution in Learning," January 23, 1993). The curriculum enhances the development of at least the seven different, equally important, kinds of intelligence identified by Howard Gardner: interpersonal, introspective, spatial, bodily, musical, verbal, and mathematical (logical). Most schools and achievement tests only acknowledge the last two types of intelligence on Gardner's list (Gardner 1985).

For children to achieve potential, the point is not to evaluate *which* intelligence is more important, or even more valued by society. Rather, when that child (or anyone) has the opportunity to excel at any of his strengths, then the positive esteem and learning from that experience will carry over into other tasks also. This fundamental pedagogy was demonstrated by the Pace School students, who became motivated to engage their academic goals once they found success helping the handicapped students. The ABC special quoted a boy at the Key School who began each day with trumpet lessons: "When I take music class, I feel better the rest of the day." Another benefit of the Key School philosophy is that students recognize the varied gifts of their fellow students in many different areas.

The other examples of "Common Miracles" in public urban schools were truly heartening because they did not depend on any magic solution or extraordinary financial resources. Daniel Webster school in San Francisco, a school with many poor and immigrant families, changed from the "worst" school to an "accelerated" school when the staff sought out the best elementary programs in the country, including many developed for "gifted" children, and introduced them to their students, with the highest expectations. "When educators treat each child like a surprise, instead of trying to label them or strictly dictate what they'll know and be able to do, virtually all kids can become enthusiastic learners."

TURNING ON LEARNING IN MIDDLE SCHOOLS

Let's return to our interviews with gang members and recall what they said about junior high and middle school. Kahlil reported that he started hanging with gang buddies from fifth grade on. Darryl said, "It was girls and violence, seventh and eighth grade. I didn't learn a thing." Ray echoed those reports: "I probably did pretty good to about the sixth grade. Then I started hangin'." Kahlil said of junior high school, "I didn't like it at all. I couldn't read very well."

These are the words of those who dropped out of the system and gave up hope. Most urban youth try to stick with the system, however poorly it serves them. As we mentioned in Chapter 2, the mismatch in junior high school is between young adolescents' needs for group bonding while also challenging adult authority and the needs of the large, factory model schools to keep order and assert authority. As gang violence and effects of family instability reach into ever younger school grades, that gap becomes more and more evident.

As William Glasser put it in *Control Theory in the Classroom*,

Secondary schools have many more losers than winners because there is more failure, more competition, more emphasis on memorization and less on thinking than there is in most elementary schools. It is this lack of access to power in the academic classes that is so frustrating to students because it comes just at the time when students are beginning to experience the increased need for power which is part of their normal course of development. (1986, 63)

The Carnegie Report of 1989, "Turning Points: Preparing American Youth for the 21st Century," called for sweeping middle school reform aimed especially at helping the 7 million children ages ten to seventeen identified as "at risk" of becoming troubled, unproductive or even dangerous adults. The Report recommended creating smaller communities of learning—each "house" or school within a school consisting of 200 to 300 students grouped in learning teams of students and teachers with close advising for individuals. An interdisciplinary core curriculum should emphasize critical thinking, personal values, and a concept of health and community service. Tracking would be eliminated and replaced by cooperative learning. Schools should participate in promoting better health and fitness (reported in "Help for At-Risk Kids," *Time*, June 26, 1989, 51).

The key to restructuring secondary schools to better meet the needs of students is the intelligent use of computer technology, both for reorganization and for creative individualized instruction. Computers can turn on learning. While these arguments may seem far away from the concerns of the gang members we spoke to, transforming the curriculum and the setting in which it is delivered will go a long way toward making secondary schools more joyous, productive and relevant places for young people to learn and grow.

First, the setting: the most creative structural reform to encourage more flexibility in secondary schools was proposed almost thirty years ago by Dwight W. Allen, Dean of the UMass School of Education and his former colleague from Stanford University, Robert N. Bush. By breaking time and space down into small units, or "modules," and by using computer power to create and monitor individualized educational menus, tremendous flexibility could be achieved in a school schedule. For example, both large-group lectures (or movies) and one-on-one tutoring sessions could be easily scheduled. In between would be cooperative learning teams, small discussion groups, lab partnerships, and individualized computer-aided instruction. The time modules could range from ten minutes to ten times ten (an hour and forty minutes) or more.

Teachers, thus, could design learning experiences for optimum group size, length of time and space use. Movies or visual arts could inspire and entertain 200 students in an auditorium for an hour or more. Individual work for twenty students in the language lab might last thirty minutes evaluated by individualized computerized performance criteria. Science students might work together in teams of three or five in a lab on a cooperative learning task, later comparing their results with other groups.

When a flexible schedule is combined with a differentiated staff—such as school managers, curriculum designers, teachers, paraprofessionals, student teachers, neighborhood parents and volunteers, older student mentors, and adjunct teachers from business and other professions—then the full creative, educational resources of a community could come together.

To come down from the blue sky to urban school reality, what is most crucial today for urban adolescent youth is success in school and support for their group identities. Here, the curriculum can be a help or a hindrance. Traditional secondary school curricula only recognize the winners and losers model; material is presented and then regurgitated. Those who remember the most get A's, and the rest get lower grades. Time spent sitting in the classroom is the primary criteria for advancement.

Educators now recognize that achievement and competence in the real world, even in higher education, depends upon many other kinds of criteria and evaluation. For example, achieving "performance criteria" means demonstrating that a certain task has been completed, regardless of time spent on task. We issue drivers' licenses based on performance criteria. Many curriculum units in languages, math and sciences readily lend themselves to performance criteria and computer-aided instruction and evaluation.

At a school in Georgia, reported in the program "Common Miracles," seventh graders who had been held back as much as two years in elementary school were able to catch up and move into eighth grade with their peers. They accomplished this through 270 carefully designed performance criteria assignments completed over the course of one year. They understood that they could finish three years in one if they kept on task. Being able to catch up kept them in school. They had a second chance.

In the world of work, many problems and tasks require success-ful teamwork. The ability to work with others can be as important as individual achievement. Cooperative learning curricula simu-late such real world challenges. Cooperative learning is particu-larly effective in middle school grades when peer group interaction is of highest importance to students. The fundamentals of coopera-tive learning are:

1. Positive interdependence: division of labor, dividing resources/mate-rials, different roles, joint rewards.
2. Face to face interaction.
3. Individual accountability.
4. Interpersonal and small group skills. (Johnson et al. 1990)

The famous work of David W. and Roger T. Johnson of Minnea-polis in cooperative learning has been adapted to urban gang dynamics. "Gangs provide their members with membership in a 'team,' attachment to peers, a sense of belonging to something greater than themselves, caring and committed relationships, mu-tual goals to which each contributes, a social life, participation in joint rewards and celebrations, and importantly, desired social and personal identities" (Johnson and Johnson 1993). All these qualities can be turned positive, and it is clear that educators in middle schools have to meet some of these needs, through the curriculum and through sports and other extra-curricular outlets.

In Chapter 4, "Sam" said pretty much the same thing about why his peers join gangs: "It's like family. A sense of power. Makes them somebody. It's the way you live. Gang members are your role models. All you got to live up to. An O.G. makin' money—doesn't have any job. Just on the street selling drugs." In order for coop-erative learning groups to begin to compete with the allure of gangs, Johnson and Johnson believe they must include the follow-ing conditions:

- cooperative learning must dominate each student's day, being used 60 to 80 percent of class time

- long-term cooperative base groups, composed of students and faculty, must be formed the first year that students enter a school and continue until they leave

- positive interdependence must characterize the structure of the student's activities in small groups, classrooms and base groups

- the students must be taught how to resolve conflicts constructively

- the students must function in base learning communities (Johnson and Johnson 1993).

No curriculum reform or structural change alone can draw students away from gangs or make up for family problems. However, a positive and helpful structure within a school setting can make the efforts of a caring teacher and other adults far more effective and easier to implement.

Computers—instructional technology—hold the key to turning on learning for middle school youth. A February 1993 article in *Electronic Learning* summed up that philosophy in its title: "Technology and the New Middle School: Ensuring Student Success." In fact, the Carnegie report *Turning Points* (1989), called middle school the last chance for students to succeed or fail, and said schools should "encourage students who fall short of success to try again and again, using every means available, to see that all students succeed." The creative use of computers could turn that prescription from a recipe for torture to a chance to finally connect to the pride of accomplishment.

The HOTS-Math software programs take that challenge head on and design the level of their problems to be difficult enough to frustrate students, but to lead them on toward finding their own solutions. Specifically, students experience the hard work of intellectual frustration followed by the pride of achieving a difficult task. HOTS are computer games designed for youth to discover their own learning skills. Their author, Stanley Pogrow at the University of Arizona, calls them "incomplete teaching." Students receive just enough introduction to get interested. They have to get more information from the computer. In "controlled floundering," they "fail" initially at something that is very interesting. Teachers help out only by asking questions. The students use the computer games to create their own successes.

So, what junior high school students used to call "cheating" becomes cooperative learning. And computer games, which they used to cut school in order to practice, now become a respectable part of the math curriculum. Successful use of technology inspires active learning. The students boast, "I know how to get information—how to learn." The teachers are learning too. They are transformed from a "broker of information" to a mentor to students, researcher, and collaborator (ABC, "Common Miracles").

In Louisiana, an entire district, Calcasieu Parish, with almost 10,000 students and thirteen middle schools, has embraced the new middle school movement with cooperative learning, heterogeneous grouping, and hands-on access to technology. In nine week cycles, students visit computer labs fifty minutes a day, where they learn in conditions that simulate high-wage, highly skilled jobs: robotics, computer-aided manufacturing, systems simulation, word processing, publishing and computer art. The opportunities give them real world motivation and opportunities for a feeling of mastery (Maggie Hill "Technology and the New Middle School: Ensuring Student Success," *Electronic Learning*, February 1993, 20–27).

Emoting about the present and future joys of computer-enhanced learning should be tempered with a warning that inequalities between urban and suburban schools could be increased through new technology. In "Separate Realities," published in *Macworld: Personal Computers in Education* (September 1992, 218–230), Charles Pillar described his survey of computer use in many schools, in suburbs, inner cities and rural locales: "After I visited inner-city, rural, and suburban schools in various parts of the country, and after discussions with scores of teachers, students, and schools administrators, an inescapable conclusion emerged: Computer-based education in poor schools is in deep trouble." For every story of some success in utilizing technology, there are hundreds of stories of computers sitting unused because staff are not trained, or because of security problems. In a Miami school that refused Pillar's requests to visit, one official told the truth: "If you talk to the kids, they want so badly to have things the way they are supposed to be. They want a Coral Gables. They want the classes to teach them something. They want to come out of there being something."

HIGH SCHOOL: WINDOWS TO THE FUTURE

Most of what we observed about young adolescents in middle schools and junior high schools also applies to high school students—with one big difference: by age fifteen or sixteen, young men and women are looking through windows to their adult futures. The role of follow-the-leader, what I call "pathfinders" now leads out of childhood and into adulthood. For the gang members I interviewed in Chapters 4 and 5, this path often lead to a dead-end. Darryl related, "I just wasn't high school material." Revealingly, Kahlil said he actually tried a second time to succeed in school: "I dropped out in tenth grade. Then I went back and tried to finish. But it just wasn't my thing any more."

At Westside Study Center, I worked with this age group of young people—fifteen to eighteen year olds who had left high school when it no longer welcomed them or had any relevance to their lives. In every case, however, when the community could create constructive alternatives, whether studying for a G.E.D. or work apprenticeships leading to satisfying employment, gang members chose a positive alternative. Similarly, the Pace students, mostly high school age, when experiencing the satisfaction of helping handicapped children, began to set higher educational and work goals for themselves, what I call "buying into the system."

Other researchers at the Gang Conference in Orlando reported similar motivations in the gang members and former gang members they interviewed. In Milwaukee, John M. Hagedorn of the Urban Research Center at the University of Wisconsin interviewed over 100 of the older founders of Milwaukee's original gangs. He found that by far most of the "homeboys," expressed conventional, mainstream attitudes about their goals. They wanted "a steady job," to "settle down and raise a family" and to "buy a house and a car." They felt selling dope was immoral but said, "I have to survive." They expressed that conflict in their unwillingness to sell dope to children or pregnant mothers. Despite their American dreams, the homeboys lived in an economic merry-go-round. Only 20 percent of blacks versus about 80 percent of white young men in the survey were employed. That employment was sporadic. Fifty-one percent of the jobs lasted less than six weeks. The average legitimate annual income was $2,023.

Hagedorn's findings in Minneapolis, then, were completely consonant with mine in the Los Angeles area. The "positive conclusion" is that the greatest problem is the economy, not the young men themselves. The "negative conclusion" is that as long as no jobs materialize for these youth and schools continue to push them out, prisons will take them in in rapidly escalating numbers. When Hagedorn asked the gang members what they most regretted, they answered: first, ever being introduced to crack cocaine and, second, dropping out of school.

Looking at high schools from a broader, national perspective, beyond the problems of inner cities, we find widespread dissatisfaction. In 1984—and times have turned worse since then—Goodlad asked thousands of students and parents at the three school levels of elementary, junior high, and high school how well they were doing and if they were satisfied. The percentage doing "well" and "satisfied" with school dropped from 73 percent in elementary, to 66 percent in junior high, to only 57 percent in high school (Goodlad 1984, 76). In another famous study of high schools from about the same time commissioned by the National Association of Secondary School Principals, Dr. Theodore Sizer concluded that public high schools have changed very little since they were founded in 1890, and that we can do better than continuing to operate a school designed when Henry Ford's Model T was new. We need to re-examine the old assumptions of promotion based on time spent in class, age grading, and involuntary education (*NASSP Bulletin* October 1983, 33).

Like it or not, fifteen year olds in today's society are almost adults. Many of their needs are adult needs. Their high school experience should reflect broad, appropriate choices. Learning experiences should come from individual motivation and clearly relate to young adult life goals. Apprenticeships, an old idea making a comeback, can be used within traditional settings and in nontraditional settings.

Within the school curriculum, apprenticeships can mean learning abstract concepts through watching, following and participating with someone who has mastered the desired skills and concepts, whether a teacher or fellow student. Beyond the academic curriculum, apprenticeships can be provided by community businessfolk, professionals, parents and other caring adults in real work settings which can lead to future careers. Pace and Westside both relied on apprenticeships and the motivating roles of "path-finders."

Let's return to the perspective of youth gangs in contemporary America. Many of the motivations for joining gangs are positive. Those motives were no different from our "Lucky 13" social club. We got together and spun dreams and pondered the meaning of life. Sadly, inner-city youth today have in some cases given up on life itself. Older gang members buy younger members their ceme-tery plot tags to wear around their necks as part of their initiation.

According to Professor Richard Goldstein of Syracuse Univer-sity, who spoke at the National Gangs Conference in Orlando, at least five of the hundreds of gangs are pro-social. With a national agenda to save urban youth, many more could become positive.

As Dr. Deborah Prothrow-Stith suggests, we must approach youth gang violence as a national crisis in public health. She finds hope in the solid success after thirty years of the public health campaign to diminish cigarette smoking. Perhaps the same can be accomplished for youth violence, when we approach the problem as a national epidemic. Already, some schools and communities are working successfully on "violence prevention" curricula.

That this epidemic reaches far beyond young black males in inner cities was illustrated in the *Time* magazine cover article of August 2, 1993: "Big Shots: An Inside Look at the Deadly Love Affair Between America's Kids and Their Guns." Going under cover in Omaha, Nebraska, reporter Jon D. Hull found that pre-dominantly white, middle-class adolescent boys were commonly packing side-arms in deadly, escalating games of revenge, shoot-outs and drive-bys. Buying used guns was as easy as buying "pot." His prime informant, "Doug," explained: "Parents just don't un-derstand that everything has changed. You can't just slug it out in the schoolyard anymore and be done with it. Whoever loses can just get a gun." With school out for the summer, the street pressures intensify. Said one youth, "I just don't see how I'm going to get through this summer without a gun." In American high schools urban and suburban, follow-the-leader has become a game with deadly consequences.

In Chapter 1, we reviewed the exponential increase in costs and lost productive lives in the prison systems due to mandatory sentencing laws. Based on her experience as State Attorney General in Florida, U.S. Attorney General, Janet Reno, as well as many federal judges, are calling attention to an out-of-control situation in which state budgets are busted, prisons suck vital resources from health and education, and violent offenders are returned to the streets from overcrowded prisons: "What we're faced with in America now is that the dangerous offenders are getting out because other offenders are in prison on minimum mandatories for nonviolent offenses. . . . We've got to have alternative sentences. We've got to explore preventative programs" ("Truth, Justice and the Reno Way," in *Time*, July 12, 1993, 24). Recently, the Governor of Florida, Lawton Chiles, said of this dilemma, "We can cut school costs to find the money to open up and furnish our new prisons, but then, we'll just have to build more prisons later for the children we failed to educate."

Imagine the tremendous potential resources in this country tied up in the illegal drug trade, the gang violence associated with it, and the law enforcement and prison systems that result from it! In Massachusetts, it costs $68,000 per year to apprehend, convict and incarcerate one young criminal. Nationally, the average prison costs for an individual, about $32,000, exceed the average yearly costs for a university education. Add to that the hospital costs of all the gun wounds inflicted in gang and drug dealing warfare. Add to that the costs of social workers and probation officers, police and criminologists whose work primarily revolves around illegal gang activities.

We could argue over that total figure: would it be $6 billion or $60 billion per year? The numbers are so large, they become meaningless. What is clear is that the resources tied up in the world of gangs and the illegal drug trade are enormous. Yet, ironically, the gang members themselves are not the ones who reap the largest profits. They are not the major importers of drugs. Nor are they the dealers in weapons. They fill the state and federal prisons, while the kingpins in the drug trade largely go free, and while dangerous criminals are let out in order to make room for this endless stream of young, mostly black and mostly nonviolent drug offenders. It will take some uncommon common sense and some political courage to begin to reverse this crisis situation.

YOUTH SERVICE AND TEACHER EDUCATION: NEW CONNECTIONS

We have already discussed the declining participation in higher education of minority youth, despite the fact that larger numbers are graduating from high school. A National Agenda To Save Urban Youth will have to address that problem. One partial solution, already passed by Congress, is the National and Community Service Trust Act, where high school graduates can perform national service in various roles and receive financial support for college in return, like the G.I. Bill in a broader context. This program and others like it could help meet critical national shortages for low-cost personnel in health care and human services. Young people could provide valuable services for the elderly, retarded and handicapped, for pre-schoolers, in peer education projects, in recreation, and in areas of counseling, probation and community police.

At the same time, national youth service programs should bring together young people from many different backgrounds, as now happens in military service. Mickey Kaus, in *The End of Equality*, proposed national service as an important institution to preserve the eroding democracy in our public spheres. As the gap between rich and poor, between inner city and suburb, and between public and private seems to widen inexorably, governments should make efforts to strengthen institutions where democratic interaction still takes place—such as public schools, museums, universities and parks. National youth service will help democratize a nation rapidly losing its common spaces and places.

The May 1986 Carnegie Report, *A Nation Prepared: Teachers for the 21st Century*, made many proposals to strengthen teacher education and transform teaching from "occupation to profession." A key background to the recommendations included structural changes similar to the differentiated staffing models we reviewed in the section on middle schools. A future teacher for a differentiated staffing model would receive progressive, career-long educational training and retraining at professional development sites where students, teachers, and teacher educators would conduct research and problem solving together.

One proposal, which Massachusetts has adopted, called for eliminating the undergraduate education major and instead having all teachers first take an academic major. This would be followed by a certification year or a Masters Degree in Education. The combination of better pay for teachers, better pre-professional education, higher standards of accreditation, clinical research and better linkages with universities will probably all improve the professional status of teaching. However, critics have pointed out that those strategies will exacerbate the already critical crisis of a shortage of minority teachers in American schools.

Antoine Garibaldi, of Xavier University of Louisiana, pointed out the dangers of the Carnegie recommendations in a paper presented at the 1987 American Educational Research Association Convention (April 20–24) in Washington, D.C. The most serious problem, as cited already, is the decline in enrollment in college of minority high school graduates: "It is fruitless to talk about increasing the numbers of non-white students in college unless concerted attempts are made to help the masses of children in metropolitan school districts matriculate through and succeed academically in elementary and secondary schools."

We must address the role of historically black colleges in preparing minority teachers for American classrooms: Black colleges accounted for more than half of all of the nation's black baccalaureate degrees in education. Will those students become teachers under the new requirements? Most of the historically black colleges (HBC's) do not grant graduate degrees in education. Traditionally, the most able black scholars have gone to graduate school in fields other than education, as has been true for nonminority graduate students as well. Raising graduate standards could suddenly disqualify a huge percentage of potential minority educators. "It is indeed difficult to envision more students, regardless of race, flocking to obtain a teaching credential with an added year of study unless some other conditions are met first. Those conditions quite simply are higher teaching salaries in the nation's schools and some financial subsidy from the federal/state governments, the college or university or foundations such as Carnegie. The issue here is clearly not race, but the ability to pay"(Garibaldi "Black Teachers and Reforms," *Detente to Disdain: A Minority View of the Holmes and Carnegie Reports,* AERA Convention, April 20–24, 1986, Washington, D.C.).

In summary, the greatest impediments in American teacher training programs today are (1) lack of reality-based training and the understanding of racism, and (2) a shortage of minority teachers. Much of the text of this book is directed toward the first problem, the lack of understanding of racism. Sadly, in the years since the early 1970s when I began in the field of education, people's general understanding of racism has taken a step or two backwards. For the second problem, fewer minority teachers, we have presented data that the shortage is becoming greater as time goes on. Without some concerted national effort, that shortage will continue.

At the University of Massachusetts School of Education, we have embarked on the first of what we hope will become many cooperative ventures between public state universities and historic black colleges. At Harris-Stowe College in St. Louis, two formerly historic black and women's colleges have combined into the Missouri state college system. The University of Massachusetts at Amherst was the land grant college in Massachusetts for research in teacher training and agricultural education. From these proud traditions in education, the two institutions can forge a new partnership: a cooperative venture for future teachers from both institutional settings. Predominantly African American teachers in training who have completed their undergraduate education in Missouri as well as some faculty seeking higher degrees, will come to UMass for graduate studies in education. At the same time, masters in teaching candidates and semester exchange undergraduates planning to be teachers can experience urban internships in the St. Louis schools, organized through Harris-Stowe College.

This type of educational and cross-cultural exchange could be repeated dozens of times throughout this nation. There are fifty plus land grant or public universities that began as teacher and agricultural extension institutions in every state and territory. Their historic black counterparts exist throughout the South, West and Midwest. The logical solution to the dearth of African American undergraduate students and to the great shortage of minority certified teachers is to forge these partnerships between historic "cousins." In many ways, the goals and histories of these institutions are already complementary—yet one was white and one was black. The time has come to capitalize on this great formerly "racist" resource of separate higher educational institutions. The gains in reality-based teacher training and in dealing with racism will be mirrored by the gains in future minority teachers.

BEYOND RACISM: A CURRICULUM OF LOVE

The problems we identified in public schools and the proposed solutions, drawn from a wide variety of examples, could be summarized as a call for a curriculum of love: love of self, expressed in confidence and self-esteem; and love of others, found in meaningful learning and work. Self-esteem and purpose are both necessary for human achievement and happiness. One without the other is not enough. No matter how well an innovative curriculum is designed, if a student lacks the confidence to try to learn it, then the ideas will fall on deaf ears. On the other hand, if a confident and highly motivated student is fed the thin gruel of minimal expectations, without imagination and challenge, then the result will be frustration and educational starvation.

"The Hope Factor" means more than just individual fulfillment through education, employment and success in material terms. Without purpose, work and service to others—such as Pace students discovered—material success brings just another step in ultimate frustration. So values—what I'll call simplistically, "love"—are an essential part of a young person's education. We need to have this reality there at every level of learning, from *Sesame Street* to graduate school.

In elementary school, children from every race and background need to feel loved and accepted as a prerequisite for learning. In middle school, "tough love" is needed in the form of schools that honor the turbulent individual changes and group bonding of adolescence while offering exciting intellectual challenges. By the high school years, students' love of self should have expanded to include service to others. Even at this late age, and even for gang members, self-esteem can be revived and strengthened through meaningful help of others. I call it the curriculum of love. It's as simple and complex as "The Hope Factor."

Most older gang members or former gang members tell us, "This isn't what I wanted for myself, or for my children." We have to rebuild urban America from those glimmers of hope not yet extinguished. Why couldn't the young people I interviewed stay in school? We have amply documented the ways in which urban schools do not meet the needs of black youth. Although overriding problems are economic—the overwhelming lack of jobs for black male youth—schools cannot abdicate their crucial role in the social order. In the short run, the problem is jobs, jobs, jobs; in the long run, it's education and jobs. But, as one discouraged street youth observed, "It's the 90s. Don't nobody try to care what's going on."

Westside Study Center was a response to the failures of urban education in Pasadena, California, a small city similar to many mid-sized American cities in its problems. Westside ought to be revisited as a model that was more inclusive than any solutions being proposed today. At Westside, everyone got involved, black and white, parents and students, gang members, police and business leaders. It became a total community commitment. The proposal for youth national service contains some of Westside's elements, but it has to go beyond Job Corps or the traditional social work role of drop in and ease your conscience. A truly interactive plan would offer significant roles for both urban youth and for college youth. Both would find their worlds enlarged and enriched.

Why are American citizens tolerating the carnage and dashed dreams on city streets? Is it because so many of the victims are young black men shot or wounded by other black men? Has indifference towards black unemployment, poor housing and poor health lead to indifference toward the loss of life itself?

In Florida, recent random robbery-murders of foreign tourists shocked the world. Headlines in Germany and England screamed outrage that the world's most free and affluent society has gone savage at its core. One law enforcement official in Tallahassee protested that the English tourist murder was the first murder on his beat this year. But, he had omitted an August murder—of one black teen by another.

Why should the crisis of basic survival for young black males matter to anyone else in America? Because without the functioning of the American Dream for everyone—without "The Hope Factor"—the basic fabric of our democracy will rot and shred. There is no freedom if citizens are afraid to walk the streets, travel in certain areas, or talk to strangers. There is no true communication if so many cannot read. There is no pride in accomplishments achieved if others were never allowed to compete.

This country needs the skills of every American youth to participate in the twenty-first century. We need jobs accessible and available for all. Every American deserves a good education. The American democratic covenant demands nothing less.

References

❏ ❏ ❏

American Association of School Administrators (AASA). 1983. The excellence report: Using it to improve your schools. Arlington, Va: AASA.

Billingsley, Andrew. 1992. *Climbing Jacob's ladder: The enduring legacy of African-American families*. New York: Simon & Schuster.

Bing, Leon. 1991. *Do or die*. New York: HarperCollins.

Boyer, Ernest. 1983. *High school*. New York: Harper & Row.

Brookover, Wilbur, and L. Lezotte. 1979. *School characteristics associated with changes in student achievement*. East Lansing: The Institute for Research in Teaching, Michigan State University. Brief #8.

Coleman, James S., and United States Office of Education, Equal Opportunity Division Staff. 1966. *Equality of educational opportunity*. Washington, D.C.: Government Printing Office.

Comer, James. 1980. *School power: Implications of an intervention project*. New York: The Free Press.

Edelman, Marian Wright. 1992. President, Children's Defense Fund. Speech to the National Press Club, April 14, 1992. Washington, D.C.: C-Span.

Edmonds, Ronald. 1979. Effective schools for the urban poor. *Educational Leadership* 37 (October): 15–24.

Farley, Reynolds, and Walter Allen. 1987. *The color line and the quality of life in America*. New York: Russell Sage Foundation.

Gardner, Howard. 1985. *Frames of mind: Multiple theories of intelligence*. New York: Basic Books.

Gentry, Atron, Carolyn C. Peelle and James W. Wilson III. 1991. Opportunity lost. *Connection* G:2.

Gibbs, Jewelle Taylor, ed. 1988. *Young, black, and male in America: An endangered species.* Westport, Conn.: Auburn House.

Glasser, William. 1986. *Control theory in the classroom.* New York: HarperCollins.

Goodlad, John. 1984. *A place called school: Prospects for the future.* New York: McGraw-Hill.

———. 1987. School renewal and the education of educators: The partnership concept. University of Massachusetts Amherst, School of Education *Newsletter* 1,2.

Hacker, Andrew. 1992. *Two nations: Black and white, separate, hostile, unequal.* New York: Macmillan.

Holmes Group. 1990. Tomorrow's schools. *Forum* 4,2.

Johnson, David W., R. Johnson and E. Holubee. 1990. *Circles of learning: Cooperation in the classroom.* 3rd Edition. Edina, Minn.: Interaction Book Company.

Johnson, D. W. and R. T. Johnson. 1993. Cooperative learning: Using gang dynamics to enhance learning. *School intervention report* 6, 3 (Spring).

Jones, Byrd L., and Robert W. Maloy. 1988. *Partnerships for improving schools.* Westport, Conn.: Greenwood Press.

Kaus, Mickey. 1992. *The end of equality.* New York: Basic Books.

Knowles, Louis L., and Kenneth Prewitt, eds. 1969. *Institutional racism in America.* Englewood Cliffs, N.J.: Prentice-Hall.

Kozol, Jonathan. 1991. *Savage inequalities.* New York: Crown Publishers, Inc.

Lightfoot, Sara Lawrence. 1983. *The good high school: Portraits of character and culture.* New York: Basic Books.

Little, Judith Warren. 1981. *School success and staff development: The role of staff development in urban desegreated schools.* Boulder, Colo.: Center for Action Research, Inc.

Lukas, Anthony. 1985. *Common ground.* New York: Knopf.

Mecca, Andrew M., Neil J. Smelser, and John Vasconcellos, eds. 1989. *The social importance of self-esteem.* Berkeley: University of California Press.

Nation at risk, the full report. 2nd ed. 1992. Portland, Oreg. USA Research Inc.

Oakes, Jeannie. 1985. *Keeping track: How schools structure inequality.* New Haven, Conn.: Yale University Press.

Palmer, Parker J. 1990. Good teaching: A matter of living the mystery. *Change.* Excerpted in "Teaching Excellence," from the Center for Teaching, UMass, Amherst, September 1993.

Patterson, J. L., S. C. Purkey, and V.P. Jackson. 1986. *Productive school systems for a nonrational world*. Alexandria, Va.: ASCD.

Payne, Charles. 1984. *Getting what we ask for: The ambiguity of success and failure in urban education*. Westport, Conn.: Greenwood Press.

Pearl, Arthur, and Frank Riessman. 1965. *New careers for the poor: The non-professional in human services*. New York: Free Press.

Prothrow-Stith, Deborah, with Michaele Weissman. 1991. *Deadly consequences*. New York: HarperCollins.

Reich, Robert. 1991. *The work of nations*. New York: Knopf.

Report of the National Advisory Commission on Civil Disorders. 1965. New York: Harper & Row.

Rutter, Michael, B. Maughan, P. Mortimore, J. Ouston and A. Smith. 1979. *Fifteen thousand hours*. Cambridge, Mass.: Harvard University Press.

Sarason, Seymour B. 1982. *The culture of the school and the problem of change*. 2d ed. Boston: Allyn and Bacon.

Terry, Don. 1992. More familiar, life in a cell seems less terrible. *New York Times*, 13 September 1992 1,40.

Tharp, Roland G. 1992. Cultural compatibility and diversity: Implications for the urban classroom. *Teaching thinking and problem solving: The newsletter for the thinking educator* 14:6. Philadelphia, Research for Better Schools, 1–7.

Williams, Terry. 1992. *Crack house*. New York: Addison-Wesley.

Wilson, W. J. 1987. *The truly disadvantaged: The inner city, the underclass, and public policy*. Chicago: University of Chicago Press.

Winerip, Michael 1993. America can save its city schools. *New York Times* 4A, 7 November 1993: 16–18.

Index

❏ ❏ ❏

About the Authors

ATRON A. GENTRY is Professor of Education, School of Education, University of Massachusetts at Amherst. He is the co-editor of the journal *Equity and Excellence in Education* and *Urban Education*.

CAROLYN C. PEELLE has a doctorate in urban education and has written articles and books on issues of access and equity in education.